NARCISSISTIC *Partner* ABUSE

A HEALING EMOTIONAL GUIDE TO OVERCOMING THE ABUSE OF A NARCISSIST PARTNER AND FIND YOURSELF

NARCISSISTIC
Partner
ABUSE

**A HEALING EMOTIONAL GUIDE TO OVERCOMING THE
ABUSE OF A NARCISSIST PARTNER AND FIND YOURSELF**

THERESA RECOVERY PHD

TABLE OF CONTENTS

INTRODUCTION

Congratulations on purchasing *Narcissistic Partner Abuse: A Healing Emotional Guide Overcome the Abuse of a Narcissist Partner and Find Yourself* and thank you for doing so.

We are taught from childhood to hold an idyllic view of romance. Books and movies reaffirm over and over again that real love is loyal. Real love is fixing a partner who is more than a little rough around the edges. This is a trap that we have been conditioned for, from the moment we hear our first bedtime story. There is no amount of warning that will prepare someone for the descent into madness that is falling in love with a narcissist, and there is no amount of tenderness that will fix them.

In this book, we will examine narcissists and their patterns of abuse. You will learn to spot the traits, and you will gain some insight into why they are the way they are. The patterns of abuse are almost impossible to see until someone points them out to us. Why is that? What is the difference between a normal functioning human with middle-of-the-road morals and a narcissist? There will also be an examination of the different types of abuse, and some of the techniques that they use to gain control over their victims.

This book will also be taking on the task of healing and how to come out on the other side of this trauma, wounded but whole. There are so many steps that victims of abuse may take to begin the process of taking their lives back. There is no way to undo the suffering that you've encountered, but you can and will move forward from this. Human beings are resilient creatures.

There are plenty of books on this subject on the market, thanks again for choosing this one! Every effort was made to ensure it is full of as much useful information as possible. Please enjoy!

CHAPTER 1

Inside the Mind of a Narcissist

There is a profundity to the word narcissist and the implications that lay hidden within it. Defining this word will be someone's first step toward healing. Information is power, and that is especially true in this case because the victim is choosing to no longer battle an abstraction.

Narcissus was a figure in Greek mythology who accidentally became so infatuated with his own good looks in the reflection of a pond, that he died. Long before his inevitable death, he was approached by many hopeful suitors, but he found them all to be subpar. Narcissus could only love himself, and that is the perfect place to start.

Those with narcissistic personality disorder are incapable of empathy, and this could likely never change. These individuals are entitled, manipulative, and have delusions of grandeur. Narcissistic people may also be fun, charismatic, and intelligent; this is how it's possible to end up as the victim in a relationship with an abuser. Narcissistic partners use several tricks to make those that they are involved with, stay the course. The most important first step for a victim is to identify the behavior so that they may escape and begin the healing process.

Through this chapter, we will discuss many of the dating pitfalls and symptoms that the relationship is potentially toxic. Please do not see this and believe that because a partner possesses one or two of these traits, they are a narcissist. Narcissists tend to collect these traits like baseball cards, and everyone is perhaps a little toxic. Should you read the following chapter and see a good deal of our partner in the words, then you are in an abusive relationship, and the best course of action is to find a way out.

As you read, it will also be easy to forget that people with personality disorders are still humans. They're calculated and can be violently destructive toward their partners, but they're not movie villains. Those with disorders have disrupted thought patterns. Does this mean that you need to sacrifice yourself to someone who probably is not motivated to change their behavior? Absolutely not.

Abusers will never identify themselves as such, and most of the time, they are totally unaware that anything is wrong with them. This personality type can be very difficult to treat because the abuser is never the one in distress. They will never seek help for themselves. So, what does it look like to be in a relationship with a narcissist, and how would you know if you were in one of these relationships? As a partner, you will begin to notice a cycle of abusive behavior. Patterns of anger and manipulation will begin to present themselves to you as time progresses.

Narcissistic partners will storm into the picture as Prince or Princess Charming. They're able to appear as near perfect lovers, telling the victim everything they need to hear about biting the hook. Everything they say in the beginning is a façade; nothing is real. Abusers are able to mimic these behaviors because they have observed them elsewhere. A mysterious stranger rides into town, interested in everything you care about; no one can understand you in the way that this person does. They are attractive, charismatic, attentive, and articulate. They are able to appear this way because that is how they hunt. By the time the victim is aware that everything is a lie, they are already held fast on the web.

If you have ever witnessed an abusive relationship through the eyes of an outsider, there are always hushed whispers asking why the victim stayed. Why didn't he or she leave when they had the chance? Others are also quick to assert that this sort of situation would never happen to them.

Trauma bonding is part of this equation. Narcissistic abusers are masters at manipulation. They create an intense bond with their partner by alienating them and then breaking down their resolve with extreme emotional chaos. Abusers will wash over their partners with a sickly-sweet brand of fake love and affection. This is referred to as **love-bombing.** After love-bombing you can expect an onslaught of depreciation. The abuse is made of twisted and callus insults, meant to break down the self-esteem of the victim. There may even be physical violence. After experiencing such an exhausting back and forth, they seek comfort from the only person still left in their life, the abuser. The victim is both terrified and in love, and this manipulation on behalf of the abuser creates an almost addiction like effect that is called trauma bonding.

Signs that You're Involved with a Narcissist

The Charm: Narcissists have this fog of charisma hanging over them, perfumed with the sort of attention that you have been craving. Falling prey to this superior hunter is as easy as apple pie. You want to find love, and you're looking for attraction. These abusers use our desires against us, almost as a form of camouflage, to cover the behavior that would otherwise be setting off red flags.

The Stare*:* Physical cues also exist to aid in the detection of narcissists, one of the most notable being the stare. When an abuser has just met a victim, their eyes turn into intel-seeking laser beams. The narcissist has a remarkable knack for remembering even the smallest pieces of information. Many victims have mentioned noticing an intense stare that makes them mildly queasy. This deep gaze feels as though you're sized-up. You're the prey.

The Interview*:* When a narcissist has found their next mark, the first thing they require is information. In order for someone to pretend that they are your soul mate, they must get to know your soul. If infatuation were not playing a role in blinding the victim, this would feel suspiciously like an interview. Abusers need to know all of the taste-making details about the new target. They will ask question after question to obtain the data that they're after. Unfortunately, this can appear as though someone has taken a unique interest in your life. In reality, data mining is just to build ammo for the round of pretend they are about to engage in. Should they receive any information that is juicy enough, then it will be stored away and used against the victim when they least expect it.

The Tearjerker*:* The prevailing science tells us that narcissists are not born; they are made. Conflicting theories exist as to what happens in these individual's early lives that cause them to make the switch. There is some speculation that this change can be born from childhood trauma. Regardless of if their past is dark or not, an abuser will always approach the prey disguised as a victim. They want you to see them as a downtrodden hero, who has risen from the ashes of their past like a phoenix. You are much less likely to suspect that someone who has endured a deep sadness, could possibly be calculated and untrustworthy. No matter how unsettling their childhood was, there is an ulterior motive in their retelling of it, to you.

The Steamroll*:* Narcissists are experts at using guilt against their partners, and this includes the silent treatment. Abusers will use this withholding of communication to break down physical boundaries, from the very beginning. Should the victim want to grow trust before physical intimacy is brought into the equation, the narcissist will steamroll this plan with emotional warfare. Abusers want to push the boundaries of their partner in any direction that they can. There is no respect for the other party's reservations.

The Quick-Start: Abusers will jump immediately into planning for a future with the victim. They waste no time in accelerating the relationship past the point of comfort. It is very easy for a victim to ignore this sign, because who doesn't want to be swept off their feet? Narcissists will often speak about marriage and starting a family with the victim. This is a tactic used to further bond the victim to the idea that they are going to be in that relationship forever. In a healthy relationship, time is used to judge the quality of the match. In a toxic relationship, the abuser will push forward with no regard for the victim.

The Tie Cutter: One of the very first signs that you're romantically involved with someone abusive is their move toward isolating you. Individuals with a narcissistic personality disorder will pick fights with the victim's friends and family. Abusers will do anything they can, to ensure that your attention isn't divided when it comes to them. Abusers will also make sure you understand how toxic everyone in your life is, everyone except them. A narcissist will always make sure that their needs are being met. They want to be the only person receiving your attention, and that is what drives most of their interactions with your loved ones. An abuser will also prefer that you feel as though you are completely dependent upon them because dependence will make it much more difficult to escape.

The Only One that Matters: Abusers seem to have an image of themselves that seems unshakably good (it isn't). They're desperate to validate that image constantly. Those that are beginning to come around to the idea that they're trapped in this type of relationship will be able to think back on their partner's self-important behaviors for clues. A narcissist is someone who only cares to talk about themselves, and they are one-sided conversationalists after the interview phase. The conversation is about what they enjoy, what they've experienced, and what they want. Your day does not matter to them, because they also had a day and they're more important. If you're ever in the process of trying to diagnose a past (or current) relationship, think back to all the times that you've spoken to them about your interests and how those conversations were received.

The Domestic Terror*:* Abusers will create an atmosphere of fear within the relationship, and they have the ability to weaponize your words against you. The victim will walk around with a general sense of unease, all the time; a feeling in the pit of one's stomach that something is very off. This dance on eggshells is because a narcissist will use anything that is said, as a means by which to start a fight. Compliments? How dare you compliment them in this area and completely ignore how great they are in this other area? Stresses? They are stressed out enough, and you're not helping that by adding on to it. Angry with them? How dare you be angry with someone who is going through so much right now? There is always a reason for them to pick an intense fight. This subtle word roulette will result in the victim always raking over their words again and again. It's an environment filled to the brim with stress, chaos, and panic that never takes a moment's rest.

The Psycho Ex*:* According to an abuser, every past relationship that they have ever had, has dissolved because of their "crazy" ex. This is a giant red flag that reads "NARCISSIST." Abusers are unable to accept any blame that they may deserve, for their part in past failures. This sentiment extends, especially to past relationships. They are more than pleased to tell you all about the evil ex who splintered apart their bond with hysterics. Abusers also use these criticisms as a method to shape the new victim, by using stories about their ex and traits they found unattractive. It's the suggestion that someone that was the same position that the victim is currently in should advise the victim on how to be more palatable. Narcissists use ex stories as an example of what not to do.

The Unreliable*:* Narcissists are incapable of looking at any situation from another person's point of view. We know this by now. We can use this to make sense of our next clue that they are completely unreliable. This sort of person could land their dream job, and they would be late to the first day. There is no one's time that is more important than their own, and therefore they are not dependable. These individuals are also the type to fly into a steaming rage if someone were to be late to an event that is important to them. If you're in a relationship with a person who has been late to more than one of your birthday parties, it is time to take a closer look at that partnership. An abuser will make excuses for their behavior, but they will never make an effort to change. Narcissists are fundamentally unreliable, and this goes for appointments as well as promises. If you have noticed a disconnect between your partner's' words and actions, there is a chance that the relationship is hiding some more sinister issues.

The Entitlement*:* Have you ever been waiting in line at the store, and noticed another customer acting more agitated with the passing of every second? Have you ever witnessed someone screaming at a cashier for the store not carrying an item they desire? This sort of entitlement can also provide us with a snapshot of narcissistic behavior. Abusers are entitled, in every situation. The world is required to meet their needs, and if it isn't doing so, then their lives are over at that moment. Narcissists will expect that their partners and everyone else bend to their whim. This behavior can also manifest anxiety in their partners because when abusers are out in the world, the slightest inconvenience will throw them into a rage and the victim is left to pick up the pieces of battles that didn't involve them.

The Unlawful*:* We have all heard the saying, "The rules are made to be broken." This is a narcissist mantra. They roll out of bed each and every day with defiance, and they project this attitude into every decision they make. They derive joy from pushing both societal boundaries and the boundaries of their partner. They're speeders, illegal parkers, trespassers, thieves, and daredevils. When a narcissist breaks the law, they receive a rush of adrenaline and feel something that resembles pride for having found a way to skirt the status quo. That's not to say that everyone with a speeding ticket is a narcissist, but if you've ever met someone who takes joy in breaking the rules or maneuvering around the law, that is cause for concern.

The Handcuffed*:* Abusers absolutely resent authority and will take issue following the orders of a boss. This can be a major clue for a partner to watch for, although it may not affect the victim directly. There will be a grudging disdain shown toward those in positions of power, by the narcissist. These sorts of partners will argue with the police and push their boundaries at work. They will speak with condescension about situations where they were considered a subordinate.

The Contrarian*:* Narcissists will take issue with almost everything and will act contrary to almost anyone, just for fun. They willfully pick fights with their partners and are experts at twisting language and outright lying. Abusers need to feel as though, not only are they always right, but also that they set the standard for any given thing. They will argue with any instruction given and complain when things don't go well for them after they have broken the rules. They feel the desire to contest everything. Abusers will challenge things in order to feel better about themselves, and this is a theme that you will notice again and again.

The One-Upper*:* The most obvious traits should not go unremarked, so it is worth mentioning that abusive partners are habitual "one-uppers." If you are sad, they are suicidal. They will use any situation or conversation as a ladder with which to elevate their own self-esteem. There is nothing that the victim will be allowed to have as an area of interest because abusers feel the need to commandeer anything that might be a point of passion for the other partner. These individuals thirst for attention, more than they care for anything else. If you're exploring a new subject, it's either boring or something that they have already mastered.

The Mirror: Abusers speak with pride about their ability to manipulate others. In the beginning, a partner may mistake this sentiment as refreshing honesty, but in truth, it is their entire personality. In a narcissist's universe, they are the only character that matters. Everyone else is there to be played, a tool to use for their own achievements. There is no such thing as love, only pawns that may be used for their desires. It is believable when an abuser speaks about love, but if they're incapable of empathy, then what is it really? An abuser may even believe themselves when they claim that they love you, but the truth is that they love the way that you make them feel about themselves. Everything about the victim is replaceable except for their unique perspective of the abuser, which is what the narcissist is in love with.

The Only One Who Understands Me: Narcissists have trademarked the term "soul mate" and will use this affirmation to really lure their victim in. This is beyond just the normal first charm. They will make you feel as if they are the only person in the world who can really understand you. Abusers will make you feel as though they both accept and identify with every aspect of your personality. They will take measures to ensure that you believe their interests align with your own. They will make the comment again and again, that no one gets them the way that you do, and that no one will ever love you the way they do. This is straight out of the narcissist playbook, and absolutely something to be wary of. If someone appears to take on every aspect of your personality the moment that you begin talking to them, please understand this as a red flag. This is just another evil trap in the arsenal.

The Image: If the victim isn't important to an abuser, then what is? This is another clue into narcissism because the answer is their image. There is nothing more important than the way that the rest of the world perceives them. They want to be desired, adored, and envied. The purpose that a partner serves them is the appearance of being desirable. Abusers will fuss endlessly over their own looks, and they want their partners to look just as dashing. Their mind is constantly running over everyone else's opinion of them, and how jealous they must be. A normal person would see people in a crowded restaurant and barely make a mental note of it. A narcissist will see an audience, and then they will perform. It almost goes without saying that material possessions mean a great deal to these individuals. They are ashamed if they don't own the hottest car. Extreme narcissists will always dress to impress and will usually expect the same from their counterparts.

The "Feelings"*:* Abusers will use your feelings against you because they are of the belief that what you feel is completely irrelevant or it just makes no sense to them. Some narcissistic partners will do their best to imitate expressions of emotion that they have witnessed throughout their own lives, but really unlucky victims will be subjected to a partner who doesn't even try to fake support and just finds feelings to be annoying. Narcissists tend to think of themselves as above trivial things like other people's emotions.

The Drama, The Intrigue*:* Narcissists are the main characters in their own personal dramas, and the victim is a side-character. These individuals have some pretty undeniable delusions of grandeur, and this giant sense of self-importance is a sure-fire way to detect their presence in your life. They will almost always have a brilliantly written back story, and they will continue to play the voice of reason against their faux chaotic upbringing. While they march around pretending that they are the white knight, they are also causing nothing but destruction everywhere they turn. Abusers are ever thirsty for excitement and drama, in order to further the narrative that they have crafted of themselves in their own head. They view everything around them in relation to its importance to them and everything that happens, happens to add intrigue or trauma to their own life.

The Families Intuition: Victims often report that they didn't initially realize that the relationship was toxic, from their perspective on the inside. Family and friends of the abused partner often realize that something is strange before the victim. This is because of the immediate charm that the abuser displays when trying to win the victim over, even though turbulent times, the relationship *feels* like a two-way street until a closer examination is made. It can take months to realize that your partner is not returning the same interest that you take in their achievements, activities, and daily life. The friends and family of the victim often report feeling as though their loved one has changed in dramatic ways. A loss of a sense of self occurs in these sorts of relationships, which is often slow and undetectable to anyone on the inside. Those close to us are usually capable of insight that we may miss, so another sign that you've been trapped by a narcissist is to tune into the observations of those around you.

The Control Freak: Abusers will also do anything they can to have unlimited access to the victim, their most important source of affection or **narcissistic supply**. At first glance, this can seem as though you have landed a partner that will take the lead in difficult situations and take over the tasks associated with planning events, get-togethers, holidays, and vacations. Unfortunately, this is not done with pleasant intentions. Narcissists need to be in absolute control, and they will use their power to hold the victim in a state of isolation. Abusers will always land the victim in a situation of conflict with those the victim cares about, causing anxiety and extreme distress. This is because they are the main character in their own self -aggrandizing drama, and they need total creative control. The victim (and that person's feelings) is nothing more than a prop in this story.

The Greenish: The narcissist is convinced that everyone around them is jealous of their achievements and/or attracted to them. They have also trademarked phrases like "people either love me or hate me, but there is no in-between." If you are ever concerned that you have landed yourself in a relationship with a narcissist, listen to the way that they speak about others. Abusers have no time to cater to perceptions of them that don't fit neatly into the narrative that they've sewn together about themselves. It's obvious from the way that they address inconveniences as though people are intentionally creating obstacles for them out of jealousy. Listen to the way that they describe friendships and work associations, as they will always insist that others are secretly harboring an intense adoration for them.

The Cheat: Abusers also usually have issues with infidelity. They have a dire need to use everyone around them to validate their physical appearance, and that can lead to both flirting and cheating. These individuals will often make up believable excuses for their actions, in order to keep the victim in their place but will work to change nothing about their behavior. Should an abuser be called out, they will use the accusation as a chance to fly into a self-righteous rage directed at the victim. Flirting, at the very least, will usually be present toward people outside of the relationship. New people are more exciting and the more attention that they receive, the better.

The Gang: Taking a close look at a narcissist's friend group may also be telling. They are attracted to yes-men and women. They are on the hunt for associates who will see them with the same rock-star vision in which they see themselves. They keep around pawns that believe the hype, and boost the narcissists' view of their own drama. Should a friend speak up against an abuser's behavior, then they are no longer a friend. They consider contrary opinions to be the ultimate betrayal, and therefore they don't seem to keep people around for very long. They will also do anything to protect the reputation that they have carefully cultivated on the backs of everyone that they have used.

The Memory Fog*:* Gaslighting is a term that you have probably heard if you have done any amount of reading on this subject at all, but what is it and how can we use it as a tool for detection? Have you ever been in a relationship where your partner was willing to twist your words or outright lie about past conversations to win an argument? This is gaslighting and will make anyone begin to question their own sanity after a while. The abuser will change conversations in retrospect and insist that it was just the way that the words were spoken. They will pull out this dark tool as often as they can if it means that they accomplish their goal by winning the fight. Once or twice this can be difficult to detect, but after it's been done enough, the victim will begin to question their own memory. Should this ever be a sentiment that you express in a relationship, then it's time to examine the motives of your partner.

The Devil's Long-Lost Friend*:* Having a partner that agrees with everything you say would be horribly boring. We crave a certain amount of discourse, and that is how we learn about new perspectives and further our understanding of any given subject. On the opposite end of the spectrum, an abuser will disagree with almost everything that their partner says, for sport. Narcissists enjoy playing the devil's advocate to a fault. They aspire the make the victim feel silly or dumb for their positions because it's a way for them to exercise some of that fierce intelligence (in their own minds). They enjoy ripping a statement to shreds, because it is a way for them to impress upon others how witty and forward-thinking, they are.

The Clock Watcher*:* Narcissists have no concept of empathy; we know that. Another unfortunate side effect of this lack of moral compass is that there is zero patience within these individuals. They are all about getting what they what, and when they want it. Abusers find agony in waiting for anything that they desire. This is another instance of the world being out to get them. This is a character trait that will be difficult for an abuser to hide because they will be in physical discomfort every time a situation arises where they are delayed their gratification.

The Blameless: In an argument, a narcissist will never accept blame. This is another trait that will be very difficult for the abuser to hide, once they are deep enough in a relationship for fights to arise. No matter what approach is used with these individuals, there will never be enough evidence that they have done something wrong. Should your only goal be to mention a way in which their actions have hurt your feelings and you, wish to discuss ways to avoid this in the future, an abuser will take this as a personal affront. Constructive criticism does not exist, and any suggestion made for the betterment of the relationship is a challenge. In their minds, if your feelings are hurt, it is because you deserve it.

The Gut Feeling: We have already discussed how the victim can overlook red flags because they're caught up in the intensity of a budding romance. There is still a way to read the apprehension that we as humans manifest when we are placed in a situation that our subconscious deems to be dangerous. When we are confronted with abusers, some of their interactions come off as fake and uncomfortably forward. Interactions such as these cause our body tense up. There is a feeling of unease and anxiety brought on by the strangeness of their actions. These individuals produce an uncanny valley effect but contrasting with healthy human interactions instead of looks. If you are in conversation with someone that you've just met and you're vetting them to be a significant other, and your body begins to react to the way that they are speaking, run.

The Conclusion

Narcissists come from a murky part of human nature, with conflicting studies suggesting that they can arise out of both childhood trauma and overindulgence. Other studies seem to point to genetic predispositions. Narcissists are not monsters, but they are synonymous with abusers in this context, because of the havoc that they have historically wreaked upon their relationship partners. It is not uncommon for survivors of these relationships to have PTSD, and a real hesitance when it comes to trying to trust people again. For those that have made it through trauma of this nature, the examination of your abuser in retrospect can be almost cathartic. There are so many reasons to be interested in this aspect of humanity, but this is not in the interest of demonizing those with a disorder.

If you suspect that you are narcissistic, and it is something that you would like to change about yourself before you destroy another loved one, the best course of action to take is to find a therapist and begin working on these behaviors. Some psychologists believe that this is something that the individual will never be able to change about themselves, but there is evidence that narcissists can learn to mimic empathy. Other professionals believe that the individual may be able to affect change through lots of hard work toward identifying the root cause and the disruptions in the thought process.

If you are anyone other than a narcissist, then arm yourself with this information and carry it with you always. There is an even chance that you, too, could fall victim to this predatory type of relationship. Remember these words and use them to defend yourself against a wolf that can potentially arrive on your doorstep dressed as a soulmate.

CHAPTER 2

A Closer Look at the Abuse

Being in a relationship with a narcissist is unforgiving and dehumanizing. They are emotionally empty and seek their validation from superficial and materialistic means. Even the way they "love" can be a form of abuse because their partners are pushed to please them only to end up being emotionally drained by the need for more attention and more affection. They're also afraid to look in the mirror with any self-awareness. Narcissists have a chronic fear of failure and dependence. People with this disorder tend to turn their anger outward toward those closest to them, and anyone they feel may wield power over them.

On principal, they will tear down their partners because nothing will ever be enough. Nothing could possibly fill the void left by their stunted developmental growth and emotional incompetence. They must outwardly embody behaviors that mimic confidence and self-control because they lack both of these things. Narcissists are fascinating, but ultimately (usually) static characters who bring destruction and chaos to everything they touch. They are worth sympathy but sympathize with them from afar because they will accidentally abuse anyone within earshot.

In this chapter, we will be taking a closer look at the behaviors and abuse caused by individuals unfortunate enough to have this emotional disability. We will put their abuse under the microscope and use it to try to understand why they are the way they are. There is also a certain safety that comes along with understanding their tactics, and the reason that their victims tolerate the abuse for as long as they do.

Covert Narcissists

The way that narcissists have been described so far lends to the image of someone loud and charming in nice clothes, walking around and declaring how great they are to the unwilling public. It is important that we note, there is more than one brand of narcissists, and it would be detrimental to our purposes to let the covert crowd fly under the radar. Covert narcissists are much trickier to recognize.

Covert narcissists are shy and reserved. They are sometimes referred to as "introverted narcissist." These individuals tend not to fit the outward stereotype that we have built up in our head of someone projecting a metric ton of confidence. They tend to move around unnoticed, but they, unfortunately, have some pretty major defects

These individuals seek gratification through another person, whom they have placed on a pedestal. They are depressed, lonely, and lacking a sense of self-worth. You may be thinking that all of these things don't sound so bad, but this is where we get to the narcissistic part. These people all have some giant aspirations and are under the impression that they are a diamond in the rough. They believe that they are just misunderstood but much more intelligent than everyone else. They possess a lot of self-loathing, but they are also entitled and baffled as to why no one appreciates them for how special they are. Covert narcissists also have the same lack of empathy that is the narcissist brand's trademark. They believe that everyone else is boring and ignorant, and have a difficult time being interested in others.

The plan of attack for a covert narcissist includes playing on the emotions of others. They will tell long-winded stories about the injustices that they have been done, or they will speak negatively about themselves in order to gain pity and sympathy for their plight. Covert narcissists are more underhanded and passive-aggressive toward those around them, instead of being outright rude.

Covert narcissists are extremely sensitive but also very quick to be dismissive of others. In their own heads, they are more intelligent than everyone else, and it's a burden to listen to others. They see themselves as tortured victims, and no matter what anyone does, this will never change. They use anxiety as a defense for many of their own shortcomings. All accounts state that they are just as dangerous for their partners as overt narcissists. This is incorrect. They are uniquely more sinister because of the layout like a wounded animal for their prey.

Once a victim has been chosen and captured on the web, their whole existence now consists of trying to talk the covert narcissist off a ledge that doesn't exist. Nothing will ever be enough to save them, because it's all an act. They'll use your empathy against you and push you to your limits. All the while, the abuser still views you as a pawn and is not bothered at all by using every last bit of you. They pretend to waste away, and they will still blame you for not caring about them enough. Every now and then you hear a story about someone whose partner has threatened to kill themselves if they're broken up with, and that is perhaps the most real-world example of covert narcissism that can be provided. Covert narcissists are much more common, so it is intensely important to be wary of anyone that attempts to use pity as a means to get to know you.

Overt Narcissists

Overt narcissists are charming and much more likely to try and entice those around them with grand stories of their achievements. They are the extroverts of the narcissist world, and they command attention from everyone they meet. They are more aggressive than passive, and there is no mistaking the charisma. This is who everyone pictures when they hear the word "narcissist." They differ from the covert narcissists by being terrified of appearing weak. Their biggest fear is to appear dependent on anyone else.

Overt narcissists are arrogant and self-obsessed to the outside observer. They roam the world loudly tooting their own horn and letting everyone around them know of their superiority. They crave attention and feed off of the compliments that they spend most of their time fishing for. They are much easier to spot because there is nothing reserved about them.

Narcissists do not exist as perfect examples of either of these; instead, they drift back and forth as they become more actualized through society's image of them. Covert and overt are the same person with different degrees of reinforcement for their façade. If a person with no empathy is told their whole lives that everything, they do is right and they are brilliant, said the person would be on the path to becoming an overt narcissist. Covert narcissists exist because they are constantly falling short of their own self-image, and no one is boosting their ego. They feel like misunderstood geniuses.

Types of Narcissistic Abuse

Covert

Covert abuse and covert narcissism are not the same things, but it's no surprise that the word "covert" is thrown around a lot in relation to narcissism. Covert abuse is subtle and involves the abuser taking stabs at their partner through the guise of conversation. It's an insult that is directed at someone else in a very roundabout way, so that if the victim calls the behavior out, then a fight can be picked about how the statement wasn't meant in that context. Imagine that the abuser observes someone that looks similar to the victim, they may tear that person's looks apart in front of the victim. The abuser will make disparaging comments about anyone who is interested in 'x', knowing that it is also the victim's interest. The narcissist may flirt with other girls in front of their partner so that if the partner speaks out, the abuser can claim that the victim is just jealous.

This can also manifest as dangerous comparisons between the victim and another person, such as an ex. The abuser will also hold the victim up against themselves and pick apart the differences that they know will be impactful. Covert abuse may also include comments that are negative, made in a tone that is casual so that the victim is aware they are being insulted, but (again) not able to defend themselves without starting a fight.

Verbal

Verbal abuse may include covert abuse but is also much more straight forward. It's insulting, screaming, arguing, and condescension. Anytime that the narcissist uses words as a weapon (and that is a favorite), then it is verbal abuse. Narcissists are masterful at raising their voices to win an argument. They will also demean and insult their partners, just to maintain their dominance.

Gaslighting

Gaslighting is a favorite manipulation technique in the narcissist's toolbox, and they are going to pull it out for every occasion. Gaslighting is the act of lying about or twisting the other party's words to cause them to doubt their own reality. This will often involve outright lying and usually causes the victim to begin to question their own sanity. It's uniquely frustrating to listen to someone else place words in your mouth, especially when the lie is recited with such conviction again and again.

Silent Treatment

The partner of a narcissist is not actually important to them, other than acting as home base for most of their attention needs (narcissistic supply). This means that anytime an argument occurs, the abuser has the opportunity to starve their partner of affection and acknowledgment by cutting off all communication. They enjoy watching their victims break down over the length of the silence because it's a manifestation of the power that they wield over their partner.

Emotional Blackmail

This is a specialty for narcissists. It is the use of the victim's emotions against them. It's threatening to kill themselves if you leave, evoking a sense of dread and guilt for their situation. It's threatening to do something that will really damage the victim's trust and feelings if they don't agree to lose the argument. Abusers love to use this as a tactic to maintain control because it is both effective and deeply psychological. Emotional blackmail will slowly wear away at their partner's sense of stability. It tends to involve no-win situations for the victim.

Regular Ol' Blackmail

All of the sensitive information that they have learned about the victim during the interview process is now locked and loaded. They will use this tactic to hold your own traumas over your head for personal gain. Narcissists will attack your character with mistakes that you have made in the past and informed them of. Abusers are incredibly resourceful when it comes to tearing others down, and they aren't the type to pull punches.

Manipulation

This is a tactic used by the narcissist to exert control on their victim and can be very subtle. Manipulation is when an abuser attempts to curve the victim's behavior or produce guilt with the use of indirect language. It is usually exploitative in nature and only benefits the narcissist. Abusers are unabashed about their ability to use manipulation in their day to day lives, in order to achieve their desired end-result. Manipulation may include gaslighting and emotional blackmail, but there are many other methods that narcissists have available and are generally masters at creating false realities.

Minimizing

Minimizing is the tactic of discounting the victim's own experiences. This occurs so that the victim second-guesses their own sanity and does not feel validated or important in the relationship. This can occur even when the victim is trying to discuss the abuse that they have suffered at the hands of the narcissist. Minimizing goes hand-in-hand with the drastic one-upping that is symptomatic in abusive relationships. The victim states an opinion, and the narcissist behaves in an uninterested way or finds a way to void the statement made by their partner. This brand of manipulation can be very toxic because it means that one partner is chronically unheard by the other.

Violent Escalation

Narcissists are impulsive and can be very quick to anger. Their relationship partners are often left bearing the burden of this explosive behavior. Fights that would not even be a blip on the radar of a healthy relationship may send an abuser into an all-out screaming match. Abusers are accustomed to willing arguments, even if this means they must become the loudest and enraged party in order to do so.

Having a violent temper is not necessarily indicative of physical violence, but the emotional wounds that come from adapting to life in a warzone can be so serious that it has caused the victims to have PTSD upon leaving the relationship. These relationships consist of forever tiptoeing on the edge of detonating a living bomb.

Isolation

Abusers use this tactic to restrict the victim from seeking the support of their friends and family; it is just another way to create weaknesses in their partner. Narcissists will intentionally create tension with their victim's support system, the moment that they are allowed access. Many times, the victim will even be moved away from their original location for this very purpose, under the guise of a necessary change of environment for the abuser.

Should a victim ever decide to throw caution to the wind and go out with their friends, the abuser will start a fight before the victim ever leaves the house. This fight will ruin any chance of the victim having a good time, should they still wish to go at all. The victim is now sentenced to an evening sitting around their friends, miserable because of the disagreement. The victim is unable to tell anyone what has happened, out of fear. By doing this, the abuser has maintained control over the victim.

Debt

Narcissists will go to great lengths to do "favors" for their partner so that they are owed a future debt. They will create both financial and emotional incentives for the abused partner to remain, out of a sense of obligation. Please never let someone that you don't know very well, buy you anything large or take over payment for you (even if they insist).

Narcissists will also use issues in your personal life as a means to claim an emotional debt from you. For example, if a victim were to experience the death of a loved one, the abuser would use being present during this time for manipulation. They will attempt to control the other partner by reminding the victim of any perceived positive thing, in an attempt to guilt the victim into behaving a certain way. Every interaction that an abuser enters into is a transaction. Every transaction creates a currency that may be used on a rainy day, even in an emotional context.

Slander

Narcissists love to use this method of abuse and will pull it out every chance they get. Character defamation works wonders for their brand of manipulation. The first that the victim is likely to see of this is during the isolation phase of the relationship. The abuser will attempt to break apart any bonds that the victim has with anyone else. Abusers will slander the victim's friends and family to the victim, and then about-face and slander the victim to their own friends and family.

This method is also used during fights to keep the victim in a stronghold. Narcissists will specifically seek out persons of value to the victim, and then "vent" to these people about the victim's "hurtful" actions. Anyone that has regular contact with the couple will be included in this game and used as a pawn to further breakdown the victim. It is so important that we all be mindful of acquaintances tearing apart their partner's character in our presence.

The very last time that the victim will fall prey to this tactic will be upon the escape. Almost every narcissist will attempt to ruin an ex's reputation. This is music to the ears of many victims because it is the last gasp effort to engage with them. The last slander is a necessary step to leaving an abuser, and it will be the first time in a long time that the victim will be able to walk away from all of the baiting, without a word. It is absolutely a mistake to confront this behavior in the end, because the abuser will use it as a tool to maintain an open line of communication with their departed partner.

Stalking

Narcissists always want to maintain control; they are also unduly suspicious of everyone else. This can make for an ugly combination, as it means that they are obsessed with gaining intel on their partners. They will also use this as a means to keep tabs on ongoing conversations with the victim's family and friends. Even if they are not actively going through their partner's phone or following them, they will find a way to make certain that they are present when conversations with others take place. If you were left alone, then you may call for help, after all. The victim will also never be seen out, without the abuser.

Zigzagging

This method of abuse is enough to give any healthy human being a good dose of whiplash, but it is straight out of the playbook. In the first chapter, we spoke of love-bombing. Love-bombing is the over-affectionate showering of faux love, meant to disarm a victim. Narcissists will slingshot back and forth between terrible methods of verbal (or physical) abuse, and then love-bomb the victim. This is done to create a feeling that the abuser might change and to repent for whatever personal attacks are the soup du jour. Victims will hesitate to exit the relationship because promises will be made that the narcissist will modify their behavior, and things will always be like they are when the abusive partner is trying to charm the victim. The victim is in love with someone who they view as troubled, but capable of redemption. The benevolence is a lie, and the narcissist will likely never change. There is no actual love.

Abuse and love-bombing on its own are confusing, but it's listed here because it is worth noting that it can create unprecedented levels of stress for the victim. The relationship becomes an environment of tension and almost nothing else. The constant seesawing of affection will cause the victim to wake up every day, not knowing which of the many faces they will be met with.

Threatening

The abuser will use threats of violence or information to affect a change in the other partner's behavior. This method of abuse will generally rear its ugly head when the abuser is engaged in an intense rage. The shock value of these threats can be quite effective at disarming the victim, who is in awe that the person that they love would want to cause them physical harm. Threats often include the narcissist making suggestions of causing harm to themselves, such as suicide or self-mutilation.

Lying

Lying is a constant element of these relationships and may also be used as a direct form of abuse. Abusers often endeavor to convince the victim that they have done positive things, that they haven't actually done. Abusers will also use lying to try to erase the negative behaviors that they have engaged in, such as cheating. The lying is pathological, and such an abstract behavior to include, but it will always be present.

Faking Allies

This is a method of control used by abusers to disparage the victim. The abuser will either lie or use slander, to convince the victim that their whole social sphere views the abuser as altruistic, and the victim is the one that is evil. The narcissist will paint anyone that has contact with those in the relationship, as a point of contention or their own ally. This is a difficult concept to put into words without using examples, but the examples will resonate with anyone who has ever been on the receiving end of this abuse.

This behavior could include an abuser telling a victim that their boss has noticed how lazy they are and agrees with the abuser that they aren't good at their job. The abuser's mom has mentioned to the abuser that the victim is rude at family gatherings and doesn't talk enough. The victim's friend has mentioned to the abuser that the victim flirts with others when they are out without the abuser. All of these sentiments are usually lies or twisted words, but they serve to make the victim doubt their own reality.

Why Not Leave?

We have already addressed trauma-bonding, which is a term that first came from psychology literature about those recovering from cults. The easiest way to boil this concept down is to acknowledge that the victim is capable of being grateful to the narcissist for the smallest kindnesses. Existing in an environment that seeks to break the victim down, they become broken and desperate for a reprieve from this personal hell that is their relationship. The back and forth of an abuser, between abusing and then inundating the victim with affection, can cause the victim to really cling to the abuser for comfort. It is irrelevant that the abuser is the cause of the distress because the victim so desperately needs shelter from the storm.

Stockholm syndrome was named after a bank robbery in Sweden, during which the hostages fell in love with the robbers. Any act of kindness that the abuser shows is a glass of water in the desert.

There are also chemicals in the brain that cause an addiction-like response to these sorts of abuse patterns. The truth is that even scientific evidence points to these relationships being very difficult to escape. Everyone asks the question and the answer is because they can't.

The Brain's Response to Trauma

There are so many compelling reasons to seek refuge from an abusive relationship and make the escape. There are so many hurdles to jump over in order to start this process. It can feel absolutely impossible, but it is absolutely necessary. There is scientific evidence that now shows these relationships are capable of doing lasting damage to our brains.

The destruction begins in a part of the brain called the amygdala. It is responsible for the fight or flight response. Abusive relationships freeze the victim in a constant state of terror and tension, which means that the amygdala is working overtime. After these relationships have ended, the amygdala will hold the victim hostage to their fright. This is why so many come out on the other side of these relationships with PTSD, panic attacks, and anxiety disorders.

Evidence also exists that shows that this prolonged state of anxiety also damages the hippocampus. Cortisol (the stress hormone) can shrink the hippocampus when it is being produced in too high of a quantity. This means that these relationships also have a negative effect on our short-term memory, which is some of what the hippocampus regulates. There are so many invisible wounds that victims are consigned to, long after the length of the relationship.

Can a Narcissist Love?

Narcissists are usually the first to say "I love you" in a new relationship, but with everything that we have learned, that is a confusing statement. To someone that is incapable of empathy, "love" is not the same word that it is to an emotionally healthy person. Love to a narcissist carries no depth, even if they are able to pretend that they're romantic during the early days.

We have all seen The Matrix and heard that famous line about people being the batteries that powered the machine. If you have not seen The Matrix, don't worry, this will still make sense. In a narcissistic relationship, the victim is the battery and the narcissist, the machine. **Narcissistic supply** is the term used for the victim when they are the narcissist's method of validation.

The abuser "loves" the victim because the victim is able to supply them with the validation that they need. The "love" will last for as long as the victim is able to continue supplying the narcissist's need for attention and validation. This is not an unconditional state of adoration; this is an exchange. Should you match their desired aesthetic and be adoring enough to compliment them, then they "love" you. This does not mean that the narcissists will treat the object of their diet affection with respect, only that they will fight to keep the victim under their spell.

The first thought that occurs to someone who is beginning to realize that they're involved with a narcissist is "is any of this real"? The answer is a subjective YES but absolutely not.

According to the abuser, they care for the victim, but that affection would begin to fade the moment that the victim steps out of the narcissist's requirements for a mate. Not only would the abuser begin to take back their affections, but they would do so without a second thought to the victim. For example, our narcissist really values thinness in a very superficial way. Their partner has begun to stress-eat, and therefore gained a few pounds. The narcissist's knee jerk response will be to cheat, and there will be no remorse for this behavior, even though the abuser is the root cause.

How is Narcissist Made?

There are so many conflicting answers to the creation of narcissists. The most popular theory, when it comes to disorders, is that they are mostly caused by childhood trauma. This is no exception, as many doctors believe that narcissists are crafted from events in childhood that are too much for the young person to handle. Some disorders have the tendency of coming into existence as a form of protection, so for a child that was constantly belittled or told that they were never good enough, it is possible that they developed narcissism as a means to cope with the abusive behavior of those around them.

There is another popular school of thought that theorizes that the narcissists are created out of childhood indulgence. Around the late 1970s, a movement came about that seemed to favor the idea that children need to be praised and told that they are special. This was called the self-esteem movement. Some phycologists point to this sentiment as the beginning of many young narcissists and point to this as the reason that we are seeing a rise in the disorder.

Though we are seeing a rise in many disorders because they are far easier to learn about and diagnose, thanks to the internet. Narcissism isn't something that has just popped into existence, and we know this because they are scattered throughout out the record of mankind's history and throughout our prose. Many characters in Shakespearean works of drama appear to be narcissists. The Picture of Dorian Gray exists.

It is generally considered less cut and dry than one thing is the trigger for a whole personality type. Genetic predispositions play a role. The environment plays a role. The chemical imbalances in the brain play a role. More males turn into narcissists than females.

There is also a theory that parents who were overprotective or neglectful or both, can potentially lead to the child becoming a narcissist. This disorder is not even detectable until someone is an adult, which can murky up the efforts to find a cause.

The internet and the new information age has led to some really effective ways for the narcissist to find fulfillment. They are able to take pictures of themselves and upload them for other's eyes in moments. Social media also makes it very easy to create a false and flattering narrative about one's self. The internet is the perfect tool to feed the narcissistic need for instant gratification and narcissistic supply.

We are also able to reach conclusions by logic, reason, and counseling that allow us to take a glimpse into the narcissist's childhood. Families that are competitive to a fault, wherein children can only receive praise when they perform well, they have a tendency to become narcissistic. It is ingrained in their behavior from the moment they know what words are; you must prove that you are better than everyone else forever. They are also not shown a real version of love, so they grow up without having known what love looks like. As children, they were encouraged to climb over others that they had defeated, to reach their goals. They were not taught to have compassion or to care about others. Guess what they do as adults?

Get Out

No matter how they are made, if you have come to the realization that you're in a relationship with a narcissist, then you need to start planning your escape. There are people that choose to live with narcissists, and that is usually when there are children involved. If you have the means and ability to leave, then that is the best course of action, and you are completely entitled to take this as your sign. We should go over a few things before you make your plan.

Log out of social media accounts and destroy any journals or diaries before you go. The narcissist will use this material against you, and it is best that you leave nothing to chance. There also needs to be no information around that could indicate that you are thinking of escaping.

Their manipulation can also be a huge issue moving forward, so prepare in advance. Their biggest weapon when you leave will be to slander your name in your absence. If there are mutual acquaintances, avoid the urge to explain to them that the abuser is lying or twisting the truth. This may sound counterproductive, but the truth is that the narcissist is a master of manipulation and will use this as an opportunity to make you look like the abusive party and them, the victim.

Brace for no contact and hold this ground with the abuser. If you contact them, they will inform you that you left them when they needed you the most, and you are an awful person for abandoning them in their time of need. A narcissist knows exactly where your weaknesses are and have no moral issue with breaking you down at those points. We will take a closer look at the methods that they use in the next chapter. If you suspect that you are sharing your heart with a narcissist, keep reading to see if you can identify any of these abusive behaviors

CHAPTER 3

Experiences with Abuse

Abuse is not gender-specific, but more males tend to be narcissistic than females (according to current studies). This means that individuals that are in relationships with men have a higher chance of being a victim of narcissistic abuse, in theory. In this chapter, we will be taking a look at the way that both sexes are exposed to abuse.

Female Abusers

Male victims already deal with an added layer of complication due to the fact that there is a societal stigma associated with being a victim. This is regardless of the gender of the perpetrator; it is still more difficult for men to come forward with allegations of abuse. However, female narcissists exist, and for men that are in relationships with abusive women, they receive little to no acknowledgment with representation. Women that are in abusive relationships with other women also have less coverage in popular media. The word "abuser" is just not the way that women are characterized when it comes to romantic relationships. In other areas of psychology, we tend to admit that female narcissists exist, but there is just not enough literature available for those that are involved with emotionally abusive females.

Female abusers are especially dangerous because they are allowed to skirt past our radar. Those in relationships with these narcissists are often unaware that they are being abused and controlled in the manner that they are experiencing.

One unnamed victim stated that his relationship began well enough, and everything seemed reasonable until after the honeymoon period. The abuse started slowly; she began to undermine his self-esteem by picking apart his physical appearance. She would make negative comments about nearly everything that did, calling his actions "stupid decisions." The female narcissist does this to break down the way that the partner sees themselves. She began to intentionally provoke him to anger by lying and accusing him of things that he has never done. This abuser would mention that the victim was high on drugs constantly when the victim took cold medicine or was otherwise just tired. She had become physically violent in altercations.

Female narcissists will use their sexuality to manipulate their victims because it works, and it feeds their need for attention and validation. She will appeal to you as a perfect partner— sexual and charismatic. She does this to addict men to her because she needs to use his resources as her own.

These abusers really embody the narcissistic quality of being a one-upper. No matter what you have done, the lady abuser will have done something that is abundantly more important. The female narcissists are the center of their own universe and expect everyone else to act accordingly. They crave attention and drama and will always be around the watercooler at work with the new gossip. In her own head, she is a genuinely good person and excuses away all of the behavior that does not illustrate this point.

One victim shared a story about his experience with a female narcissist. Again, there were no signs in the beginning that she was abusive. Then he noticed that she continued speaking to men that she had a romantic past while being incredibly paranoid that he was doing the same thing. She not only told him about these conversations but also insisted that he read them, even though they were sexually suggestive. The abuser held these conversations over his head so that he would know that she was desired by others. She slowly began to find fault with all of his friends and family, demanding that the time he spent with them be limited unless she was there to supervise.

When this couple would argue, she would make an effort to turn friends and family against him. She would paint him in an unfair light. She lied and twisted stories to fit her own narrative. She criticized his decision-making abilities and again picked apart his physical appearance. Her phrasing was blunt and unapologetic; if she doesn't want to do something, then there is no tone of compromise in her statements. It took this young man a very long time to understand that she was toxic because this was his first serious relationship, and they're just aren't the same resources available for male abuse victims. His entire world revolved around her desires and the things that she wanted. He eventually grew weary of trying to please her, because nothing was ever quite enough.

Female narcissists have the same physical qualities as those who are mentally healthy, but their egos will be the difference. Most female abusers will look average but have above average self-confidence. They will absolutely believe that they are the most attractive people in the room. These women take pleasure in vanity and all things associated with it: name brands, makeup, nice cars, and they will be especially keen on photographing themselves. None of this means that if someone enjoys any of these things, that they are a narcissist. Vanity will just absolutely be present in one form or another.

These ladies will come on strong but then pump the breaks in regards to the relationship. Those that are coupled up with a female narcissist will notice that they take pleasure in the mess they make for their partner by withholding affection and love. Narcissists, in general, have the tendency to become bored very quickly, and they will have a difficult time hiding this.

Women also make formidable covert narcissists, meaning that they come from a place of self-pity and victimhood. These women make a play for your compassion with a sob story. Watch out for anyone who attempts to look like a phoenix rising from the ashes, exactly two seconds after you meet them. This brand of narcissist will guilt you into giving them the things that they want. Covert lady narcissists also use a babbling technique sometimes referred to as *word salad.* Word salad is when they weave together a bunch of disjointed ideas and phrases. This will make the victim agree with their demands. This is effective because it causes confusion in the victim, and they are likely to give up their point when they do not understand the other argument being made. Politicians also use this tactic to route around questions in debates and press conferences.

Another unfortunate tick to watch for is the berating of other women. Not only will these narcissists rain down wrath on their partners, but they are also known for being vicious toward other women. If you believe that you may be dating a female narcissist, find a reason to show her a picture of your ex-girlfriend. This is best done with tact, but the relationship history conversation will have to be dealt with sooner or later. These ladies will showcase their jealousy by commenting on everything from the looks of other girls to shaming other girls for promiscuity. Narcissistic females have a unique talent for seeking out the areas of weakness and cutting others down with their causal yet venomous jabs.

Female narcissists will also be the last ever to accept blame for their actions. They will hurl excuse after excuse, and if you wade through all of that, then these lady narcissists will claim that they wronged you because you needed to be taught a lesson and you deserved it.

These abusers will also seek constant reassurance that they are the best looking, best loving, best things that have ever happened to you. They will use your weaknesses to cut you down at the knees, and in the same breath, they will require that you place them upon a pedestal. These women may also seek out validation in the form of social media. This can be a huge part of the female narcissist's life because they need attention and compliments from anywhere, they can achieve them.

Female narcissists also have a habit of dumping partners that are no longer of use to them. They turn cold and distant in the blink of an eye, and there will be no reviving the relationship. Male narcissists tend to get bored and dump but will also leave the door open for future encounters. Lady narcissists will turn and walk away as if they never knew their partner.

Women have just as much potential to be abusive as men do. Some may even argue that it is possible that there are more female narcissists than we will ever know because there is such a stigma associated with being a male victim of abuse. There absolutely needs to be a change, and more literature produced for those that are unfortunate enough to end up in a relationship with a female emotional abuser. Women are far more likely to resort to violence within the confines of their relationship also, and that is another statistic that we will never know the full scope of. Abuse is dangerous and devastating, no matter what gender it is coming from. The best thing that any person can do is to arm themselves with knowledge of the disorder so that they may better avoid the symptoms.

Male Abusers

Male abusers have the disadvantage of coverage in pop culture and psychology literature, but that does not mean that they are easy to spot by any stretch of the imagination. They have the ability to be just as cunning as the female narcissists, especially in the beginning when they are doing their trapping. These individuals also see themselves as being good people and have no concept that they are abusers. Their victims may also have no idea until it is too late.

To truly understand the dangers of narcissism, we must venture into the relationships of the male covert narcissist. These individuals do not fit the media enforced mold that mentions that all narcissists must be overflowing with confidence and extroversion. Covert narcissists will often use deceptive tactics that play upon their partner's empathy, making them numb to the manipulation and blind to the red flags.

One nameless victim recounted that she ignored a lot of potential warning signs because the narcissist acted as though they were the only person who truly ever understand her. The abuser's love bombed her to form a close bond, and then slowly revealed that he was depressed, anxious, and suicidal. All these things caused the victim to feel a sense of obligation to the narcissist, no matter how outlandish his actions became. He would physically abuse the victim, and then fall back on his magic get-out-of-jail-free-card by threatening to kill himself.

"He immediately isolated me, moving me an hour and a half away from my family and friends (whom he hated anyway). The relationship was already rocky, but he had acted in a way that caused me to feel personally responsible for his safety. He was an alcoholic and an addict, and I just naturally fell into the role of caretaker. One of his favorite ways to break me down was to inform me that he was intoxicated behind the wheel of his straight drive car, a car that I had no idea how to operate. He also found joy in speeding and driving recklessly, as he would watch me scream and cry from the passenger seat.

I had always told myself that I would never end up in a relationship like this, but he hooked me so easily. Friends and family were all worried about my safety while I defended his actions. He enjoyed picking fights with me and then pushing me to the point of screaming and crying. His mother and I had an excellent relationship, so when we would fight, he would lie and say that his mom was shocked at the way I treated him.

He would push me, and then brag that he has never hit a woman. He destroyed my belongings and hurt me both emotionally and physically. He was asking his female friends for pictures of them in their underwear and then acted aggressively with me because I had become suspicious enough to snoop through his phone. His signature move was claiming that no one knew how hellish it was to be him, citing a plethora of disorders and reiterating the desire he felt to end his own life. These sentiments would work like a charm, and I would forgive him for everything.

This sounds insane, but he was not always mean to me. When he was love-bombing me, he was so smart, kind, and witty. He was everything I wanted, and he played right into this façade. It took him threatening to take my life for me to leave him finally."

These abusers will use off-brand violence to scare their victims with the implied message. They would hit walls and throw things to send a message that they could potentially be physically violent if they wanted to.

Male aggressors will also use sexual behavior but in a different way. They will use sex as a means to degrade and demean their female partners. They also steamroll over their partner's boundaries and will pressure the victim into acts that they are not comfortable with. Male narcissists will also find it very difficult to stay faithful.

Their verbal manipulation is also different to a point, as they focus on appearing to you as a bad boy, requiring the victims to save them. They're also an injured sheep, requiring the victims to save them. They are a heady combination of danger and damage.

One victim recounted that her ex narcissist took great care to look like a Twilight knockoff, complete with cowboy boots and eyeliner. He told her about all the challenges that he had overcome and how abusive his father was growing up. He drove a very nice sports car, which was his crowning achievement. She remembered that he would often remark on how other girls were jealous of her because of his looks and his car. He would also provoke other girls into flirting with him so that he could reject them in front of the victim. She says that she felt as though a cat was putting dead mice at her feet, and it was very unnerving.

Many narcissist stories have one element in common, and it is also a fail-safe way to know that you have been involved with a narcissist. Have you ever seen a nature documentary where the lion is watching whatever leggy animal it is about to have for dinner? It's a look of predation, and narcissists will emulate this stare.

Male narcissists will also use the same buzzwords and phrases to impress upon the victim that they are special, and no one is ever going to love them as the abuser will. They will say things like "I have never told anyone this" and "you and I just clicked." These abusers have the ability to mirror your personality back to you as if you were stuck inside a real-life rom-com. One victim mentions that when they met, he seemed to be interested in all of the same things that she was. The male narcissist will use love-bombing to create the illusion that he is the victim's savior. This creates such a strong bond that the victims are willing to weather cruel and demeaning behavior.

Abusers will often attempt to injure the victim's self-esteem in subtle ways. One victim stated that the abuser would flirt with other women in front of her, and then cause a scene if she were to call him out about this. The first time she noticed this, he watched an attractive lady walk past and then turned around dramatically to insinuate that he was checking the other woman out. The victim asked him why he did that, and he made the comment that he was looking at her boots as if he was sharing an inside joke with himself. This behavior only got more frequent as the relationship went on. He would make lewd comments toward mutual friends. He once flirted with a nurse in the ICU after the victim had resuscitated him from an overdose. He was furious at the victim for allowing him to leave his wallet at the house when he has rushed away in an ambulance. His revenge was to openly flirt with the nurse in charge of his care, who also found the behavior distasteful.

The male narcissists will also make comments about the victim's appearance or anything that is important to the victim. These abusers also pride themselves on being very well-versed in making others feel confused or crazy. Gaslighting is a word that you will hear again and again in relation to narcissists. They are masters at twisting around the words of past conversations, at fitting the narrative that they aim to push.

Abusers will also attempt to provoke you into losing your cool because it makes the abuser look better if you are hysterical. They enjoy poking at the victim's weak points until the victim becomes fed up and yells something awful. One victim stated that her ex-boyfriend would accuse her of cheating on him. She was the recipient of a nonconsensual kiss from an old mutual friend, whom she pushed off and immediately told her then abuser boyfriend about. The abuser remained close with the perpetrator of the kiss and would accuse the victim of making out with his friends. The narcissist knew that this was a sensitive subject and would instantly collapse his victim into a sobbing and yelling mess.

Emotional abuse can be devastating for the victim and can take years to recover from. The fact is, that they look like us, and they move around in secret. The most devastating wounds can be those that give birth to a critic in our heads that we are never going to be able to please. Narcissists have the capacity to destroy us from the inside out, and they will do it just because they can.

CHAPTER 4

Sex with a Narcissist

Narcissists have a documented need for domination and control, so how do these behaviors translate to the bedroom? Not well, it turns out. Just like everything else that a narcissist does, sex with a narcissist is about the abuser. It is another weapon on a laundry list of weapons that the narcissists are more than happy to use against the victim.

Narcissists already have a number of behaviors that are highly suspect and may apply to every area of their lives. Harken back to chapter one where we discussed the natural daredevil tendencies of narcissists? Well, this has an impact on their sex lives also, and in a fairly predictable way. Many people have kinks and fantasies that they want to explore, but because of societal norms, they are usually wary of expressing these desires to their loved ones. Narcissists do not have loved ones and resent being told what to do by anyone. Kinks will be addressed early on, and with no regard shown for the tastes of their partner. It is not a matter of their sexual preferences being more deviant than the average person, but rather a lack of the filter that would keep sexual preferences from being common knowledge. The only influence that could potentially slow a narcissist down in this regard is their image. If they believe that their sexual appetite could cause a negative reaction in relation to their reputation, then they will keep those behaviors on a need-to-know basis.

Narcissists have this charisma about them that is charming at first and can cause others to swoon over the façade that they present to the public. There is absolutely no prince or princess charming though, and the narcissist has no love or empathy for anyone other than themselves. Even the word love carries a different meaning to an abuser because they love as long as it benefits them in some way. Narcissists will also use the word love, where they should be using the phrase "I love how you make me feel."

Abusers will also use sex as a way to humiliate the partner that they are attempting to control. The withholding of sex can be used as a perfect way to entice a partner to submit because we crave intimacy from those that we are in a relationship with.

A narcissist has no use for intimacy, and therefore sex has a lot more to do with physical release and validation. Some narcissists will use sexual encounters as a way to satiate their need for compliments and approval. They feed on the idea that they are better than everyone else and need to have this notion reaffirmed to them always. Narcissists need the affection and attention that comes with physical closeness, but emotional closeness is something that they will never be capable of knowing no matter what they say.

Consent is not a huge obstacle for abusers, and they tend to walk a thin line with behaviors that are sexual in nature. Your boundaries are meaningless, and they will outright ignore them and then make excuses for their actions later. If you are easily annoyed, then annoying you into submission will also be used as their plan of attack. Abusers will use any trick that they can in order to bend others to their will, including guilt. These are the sorts of people that you hear, making the argument that condoms decrease their pleasure and therefore they shouldn't be used in intercourse. Abusers are only interested in taking care of their own interests, and of course, this extends to the bedroom. Narcissists will use your emotional bond to them, to break down the boundaries that you may have, that go against their wishes. "If you loved me, then you would..." these statements will be dusted off and thrown in the victim's face again and again.

Covert narcissists will make comments about their partners' performance, which will lead the partner to the conclusion that they will never be good enough for the abuser. They will tear the victim down piece by piece in an effort to elevate themselves. Sexual intimacy is the most vulnerable that we will ever be, and that is precisely why the narcissists choose to strike during these moments.

There is a myth that exists around narcissists that implies that they are great lovers. In some cases, this can absolutely be true. Most of the time, narcissists make unfulfilling partners and leave their lovers feeling numb and emotionally drained. In a healthy relationship, love flows both ways, and sex is the physical manifestation of this love. It does not always mean that if you are having a lackluster sexual experience, that your lover is a narcissist. However, Abusers as lovers will disrupt this current of energy, because they do not return it to their partner. Narcissists will always be energy suckers.

Some abuse victims report that the narcissist actually began to make their body recoil at the thought of physical intimacy. This is something that they ultimately blamed on themselves at the moment. There are people who have been partners to narcissists that never reach orgasm not only because that is not an abuser's priority, but also because their body was aware of what their mind wasn't. This sentiment goes along with the feeling of uneasiness that a lot of people noticed around their partner, the narcissist is setting off physical alarm bells within their partner that something is off. Our intuition can act as a huge arrow pointing toward our abuser.

Narcissists have the reputation of being serial cheaters, and that is again because their actions associated with intimacy are incredibly shallow. They are interested in the validation, and sometimes that means seeking out new energy sources. Many narcissists go through periods where they have a long string of concise relationships, bouncing from one partner to the next. Abusers get bored easily and have no issues with dumping the old partner to seek out someone that is more exciting at the moment.

Sex addiction can be an issue with narcissists, as well as an addiction to porn. The abusers are incapable of feeling an emotional connection with their partners, so they seek out the narcissistic supply through porn and sex because it allows for the validation that they crave. This behavior can manifest in cheating and can be damaging to both the narcissist and anyone that is unfortunate enough to become their partner. They will never be able to satisfy their need for attention and compliments and will destroy everything else around them in an effort to quiet the hunger. This looks a lot like an addict who is looking for their next fix with their drug of choice. It can mean that they begin to lose the ability to perform with their partner, without there being something to make it feel edgier to the narcissist.

Another unique sexual behavior that belongs to abusers is the need to hear how well they are. Many times, narcissists will excite themselves up as the best partner you will ever have, and the most attentive lover. They thrive by being able to live under these banners in their own head, and this will leak out into their sex life with their victim. They will continuously ask if they are the best sexual partner that you have ever had, and what is the partner's favorite move that they used? They will endlessly question in order to squeeze out the compliments that they so desperately crave from their victims.

Narcissists are also similar to porn addicts who have to constantly up the abnormality in the content that they consume because of desensitization. Narcissists have this need to be above societal norms; they need to feel dangerous. The fantasies of a narcissist will continue to reflect this tendency, as they become more and more taboo. Taboo, in this context, is referring to the perception that the narcissist views popular society as holding. This means that their kinks will seemingly always change because they need always to be doing something that is more daring than the last area that they explored.

Commitment is a concept that elicits a violent allergic reaction from the narcissist. With all that, we have learned this isn't much of a surprise, but some of the ways that they will act out against the relationship out of spite may be especially traumatizing to the victim. Imagine being love-bombed so much that you have formed a strong bond with your mate. This would mean genuinely thinking that this is a loving relationship, only to find out one day that they have cheated on you with several different people. This happens a lot in the ugly world of narcissism.

Narcissists tend to have this image of themselves in their heads, that they are brilliant. They are geniuses who may or may not be recognized for their talents by society. They do not see themselves as being bound by the same societal norms that mentally healthy individuals adhere to out of morality. The narcissists even view relationships as a hindrance in some ways, and the second that their needs are not being met, they are going to discard their current partner and find someone new who will satisfy the need for glory within them.

This can also mean that taking part in a marriage can feel like jail to them, and there is little to no chance that they remain faithful. They have this need to keep themselves entertained, and this involves re-upping the narcissistic supply. Marriage can also lead them to feel as though they have settled and will never have the chance to be as free as they wish to be.

To the narcissist, marriage is just a tool to tie down their partners so that they can maintain control. Marriage will make it much more difficult for the victim to escape the grasp. If the narcissist is allowed to move around unchecked in their marriage, then they will cheat. If they are expected to stay monogamous, then they will continue to make up excuses for their behavior. Covert narcissists will lie to you, while you look them in the eyes as they have been caught red-handed. Overt narcissists will just not respect these wishes and will begin to feel trapped and bitter about the relationship. This could be a means by which to lash out and further make the partner feel guilty, for what they will call a forced relationship.

It should be said that there are some partners of narcissists who are aware that they are in a marriage with a narcissist and have decided for one reason or another to try and make it work. This is not recommended but can be achieved as long as the victim is well aware of what they are sacrificing. There are some psychologists who believe that narcissists are able to change, but mostly it doesn't matter if they are or not, because they won't. Most people that go see a therapist do so because their behavior is negatively affecting their life. Those with disorders are usually looking to alleviate the symptoms of their problems, and that is why they seek help. With a narcissist, there is no detriment to them from their own behavior. Narcissists do not have the empathy to care if anyone else is affected by the way that they use people. Abusers also typically are not going to be the first ones to accept that there is something wrong with the way that they think. Narcissists also do not suffer from their own hands. Narcissists tend to be whirlwinds that cause damage everywhere they go, but they are not damaged by their own actions, so they have no reason to seek out help for their habits.

As though we have not heard enough evidence that a narcissist will cheat, there are even more reasons that they are prone to infidelity. The narcissist will use their main partner as a source for their narcissistic supply until it seems as though their partner is expecting more commitment or emotional intimacy from them. Narcissists will then form other smaller relationships and use the secrecy to set up terms that they control completely. These side relationships allow the narcissist to pump the breaks with their main partner and at the same time, experience something new and exciting. When the side relationships get boring, the narcissist will back away from them but allow for an open ending so that they may be resumed when it benefits the abuser.

Somatic narcissists use their bodies to get what they want. They use the sex drive of others as a weapon to get the things that they want. An example of this would be a younger lady that plays the role of partner to an older rich male in order to access his finances. She has no emotional connection to him but will use sex as a means to facilitate the lifestyle that she craves and has decided that she is worthy of. **Cerebral Narcissists** view sex as demeaning. They rely mostly on their words rather than their bodies. They will still use sex as a last resort to trap their partner.

Somatic narcissists are hypersexual and have no emotional attachment to their lovers at all. These are the abusers that tend to have the reputation of being a good sexual partner, in a technical way. They expend a lot of effort to look better than everyone else. Most of them love the idea of being the "other" party in an affair because they see other people's marriages as a challenge to unravel.

Somatic narcissists enjoy the use of jealousy as a tool to gain a response from their lovers. They have the same set-up as all the other abusers, one main partner and several other lovers competing for their affection. Their choice of narcissistic supply is the distress of their main partner, from seeing all of the attention that they are able to achieve from others.

Some narcissists are also known to be quite technical lovers, almost robotic. Victims have mentioned that their abusers, after a while, would perform exactly the same way every single time the couple had sex. This is another example of love being taken completely out of the equation. Sex is applied at the end of every evening like a rubber stamp on a stack of envelopes. There is no deviation to a formula that works, and after the new and exciting phase, there is no more reason to try.

Narcissists approach sex in the same way that they approach the rest of the relationships. They are invested only in serving their own interests. They use sex as a way to control, dominate, and maim. Narcissists aim to use their victim's most vulnerable moments as a way to steer the victim's actions. The best revenge against a narcissist and their underhanded tactics does not come from you or any other ex-lover, but from time itself. Looks fade with age and attachments, that, if not glued with adoration, will fall away as time rolls on and the truth comes out. In the end, the users are left to sleep in the bed that they made.

CHAPTER 5

Healing from the Damage

Healing

Escaping a relationship with a narcissist is completely necessary for the victims, there is usually no other option unless there are extenuating circumstances. The process of leaving can also have the potential to be one of the most trying moments in someone's life. It is jumping from a burning building, and then having to confront the extent of the damage that you suffered inside. There is no quick or easy solution when it comes to addressing the extent of one's trauma. We know from previous chapters that these relationships can actually cause physical changes in our brains. In this chapter, we will address some ways that the victims may begin to heal—normally after enduring these sorts of traumas, victims have no idea which way to turn next.

Rebuilding Self-confidence

During a relationship with an abuser, self-confidence takes a hit. The narcissistic partner is cracking away from the victim's self-worth more and more with every passing day. This sort of relationship has the potential to leave scars will manifest as the negative voice in the back of the victim's head, for a long time to come.

Narcissists use anything they have in reach, as an emotional weapon against the victim. Long after the abuser is removed from the equation, the victim will hear their voice of doubt echoing off the walls of their subconscious. *You aren't worthy. Everything you touch falls apart. You're a failure.* This is the legacy that narcissists have on those that they encounter. This can be a tough voice to beat because it is much easier to agree with than fight.

The victim may also notice self-sabotaging tendencies after this relationship. The victim is afraid of success because they have been let down and deceived in such an impactful way. How will they ever be able to trust their own judgment again? The first step to overcoming the residual darkness is to tackle it in the same way that you would tackle chronic depression. Start small.

There are going to be days that you do not believe that you have the strength to get out of bed, and on those days, you must be forgiving of yourself. Try your best to take a small step like showering. This will do a lot for your motivation and will give you a goal to reach. Once you hit your mark, you will receive that precious hit of dopamine and be much more willing to endure the day. If for some reason, you are not able to make it out of bed today, be kind to yourself because you need time.

Friends are a fantastic way to begin piecing your self-confidence back together. Usually, after a relationship like this, your old support network is waiting in the wings for you. These are the same people that told you that they thought something was wrong with the relationship, and then they were pushed away. Fall into friends, family, or anyone around you who sees you for how amazing you are.

Friends build up our self-esteem because they see us as we want to be seen by the world. Our support networks are able to recognize the value in us, even when we are not able to spot it ourselves. Spend as much time as you can with this sort of company, because this is an easy way to stay busy while working on your self-image when you may not even realize that you're doing so.

Random acts of kindness can also help to really regrow your sense of self. The hard truth is that narcissists seek out victims who have a large capacity for love and empathy. Abusers need a partner who will pour endless amounts of affection onto them, and those with sensitivity to such things are very vulnerable to the narcissist's charm. To learn to love those qualities about one's self again, one must practice these feelings again. It's a good idea to volunteer, or this could even be something as small as paying for a stranger's food.

Journaling can also be an excellent way to get back in touch with your feelings and can sometimes help us with the articulation of our pain. Use the journal to remind yourself why you are grateful, and what you like most about yourself. Progress will be made by documenting negative emotions, too, because this will create a way to measure your progress. Progressing along the path of healing even a little, can be a motivation all on its' own.

Ease into a routine of exercise and taking care of yourself, even if it is only motivated by revenge at first. Looking and feeling your best can do a lot for your self-image and really work to get you back on the track toward being mentally healthy after prolonged abuse. It isn't an instant cure, and it can be a lot easier said than done but acting as if you are a valuable person can do wonders for your internal dialogue.

This internal dialogue is going to be your most successful rival, as a survivor of abuse. It is imperative that victims of abuse take time for themselves to combat this negative image of self.

Schedule time each and every day to do something that you enjoy. Treat yourself the opposite of the way that you were treated by the narcissist. Sometimes it can be hard to find the motivation but remember that you had what it took to get out, and that should be celebrated in your new freedom.

This next tip is very important, do not engage with the narcissist at all. You need to win back the trust that you formerly had in yourself, and the only way to do that is to walk around with blinders on. The narcissist will spend a lot of their time trying to get you to come back or slandering your name. Do not fall prey to this because they are master manipulators, and they want you to get angry. If they are still in your life in any capacity, do not try to counter these slanders with the truth to those they are influencing. Abusers will use this as a means to turn the situation back around on you so that they look like the victim. The most important thing that anyone can do for themselves after their escape is to go no-contact. Don't blame yourself if you have already been in contact with the abuser post-breakup—just stop now.

Group Therapy

Group therapy can be very effective for healing from trauma because it opposes the idea that you're entirely alone in this situation. There are abuse survivors everywhere, no matter how many times your acquaintances tell you that they would never allow themselves to be an abusive relationship. The reality is that nearly a quarter of the population have experienced abusive behavior by a partner, in their lifetime.

As a society, we can be guilty of crafting a false narrative about happiness. It is absolutely normal to be in pain. It is normal to feel inadequate after you've been told that you are for an extended period of time. Group therapy works to remove the stigma that surrounds needing help. Everyone involved in the group has experienced similar things and has a similar level of guilt for having been abused. Knowing that you aren't crazy or alone in your fight can do so much for your mental health.

If the narcissist was successful in shredding the victim's support system, then group therapy can provide a built-in safety net. The abuser's goal in isolating the victim was to rid them of people who may object to the relationship or give the victim the strength to leave. By joining a group therapy, the victim may gain all of that back. A common misconception is that the therapist is taking turns speaking to every individual involved in the group and giving them specialized attention for a short period of time; it is much more than that. In group therapy, every member is encouraged to communicate with other members, offering advice, or similar experience. This is also a chance for the victim to use their own knowledge and experience to assist others, which will aid in healing the battered self-image.

In the same way that journaling can assist in putting words to your emotions, so can dialogue with people whom have had similar relationships.
Accepting that you have been abused can be a giant pill to swallow all at once, and it can be especially hard to define all of the emotions that go along with rebuilding yourself. Victims will exit these relationships confused and unsure of how to process all of the hits that they have taken to the idea that they've held in their heads, of who they thought they were. Listening to others who have ventured down the same path, can provide some real "a-ha" moments when it comes to articulating both the pain and the recovery.

The hidden gem of group therapy is its' aptitude for rebuilding the victim's social skills. Someone who has just escaped a narcissist has spent a prolonged period of time reciting a script in social settings. It can feel almost sinful to begin opening up about the abusive behavior because the victim has been trained never to mention this. Group counseling can provide a way for the victim to reintegrate into society, through practice on a small test-scale. You have the chance to test your people skills on a small sample of people, with the knowledge that they are enduring the same issues that you are. Group therapy can be essential for fine-tuning your social skills and relearning how to speak to others, especially when it comes to articulating your abuse. It can also function as a mirror so that you're able to perceive how others are relating to you.

Group therapy also has the potential to help the victim avoid the pitfalls of healing from abuse. Those in the group have likely made common mistakes, and their experience may serve to keep the victim from falling into the same patterns. There are so many very tempting traps disguised as short cuts, and there is always the potential to fall into some unhelpful habits when trying to heal from trauma.

These relationships can leave a person feeling empty and hollow, with a confused vision of who they are. Any brand of therapy is a great start to repairing the shattered pieces of ego. Friends and family mean well but will never quite understand the severity of the abuse that the victim has suffered. They will also never understand why it has such a lasting impact on the victim, even though evidence has shown us that abuse is capable of affecting changes in the brain. Group therapy is perfect for this brand of trauma because the weakness has been created by isolation, and without that loneliness, the victim will begin the process of healing. Group therapy is being able to walk into a room and sit down with others that have been through the same hell that you have, and not having to justify being broken by it. You will get to know people who experience mirrors your own, and you will have the opportunity to help others with their healing genuinely.

The idea of going to therapy can be somewhat intimidating, especially if you've never needed counseling before. Group therapy is a cost-effective alternative to the more traditional one-on-one counseling and may instantly erase that feeling of nervousness that is associated with speaking about one's self for an extended period of time. Those that you meet in the group will help you form your new support network, which will allow you to proceed toward your ultimate goal of healing and relearning yourself. This will be the one area of the victim's life that the narcissist will be unable to penetrate, making this small group of people sacred. You are all on the same path to changing your inner dialogues and regaining control of your lives.

Support Group

Support groups and group therapy are different in some very fundamental ways, but also share a lot of similarities. In order to understand which one you would benefit from more; it is worth contrasting the services. Group therapy is a small, closed group with a licensed therapist or two leading the discussion. There is a good deal of screening involved to determine if this option is right for the person attending. It will feature the same people, session after session, so there is more consistency with the clientele. The most important difference between the two is that group therapy seeks to change a behavior, and support groups are there to assist with coping.

After an abusive relationship and the long-term damage that it inevitably causes, group therapy would be used to address and change the resulting negative thought patterns and any self-destructive behavior. A support group would be better suited for those that find solace in finding a group of people with the same struggles that they have endured. Support groups are also open, so there is a lot less commitment, for those that might be nervous about using such a service after a trauma that induces social anxiety. In the support group, the main goal would be to speak and listen to other survivors. In the same respect as group therapy, it can really help with the sense of loneliness that the narcissist has engrained in the victim.

After being subjected to such an intense brand of abuse, it can be difficult for some people to seek help. Support groups have a casual environment that many people find more welcoming and use the meeting as a place to begin their healing. It can also be a challenge to see a therapist one-on-one, for reasons related to self-doubt.

A support group is essentially a peer-lead environment (even though there is trained specialist leading the conversation), that is much more accessible to people are fresh out of an abusive relationship. There is also no pressure to change the offending behaviors in group therapy; it is more focused on how to get past the lingering demons from the abusive relationship. There is absolutely still room for growth within group therapy, but there isn't any pressure to that end. Participants will share their experiences with narcissists discuss their struggles post-narcissist.

Group therapy is a more formal approach to changing the inner dialogue, that may be more appealing to those that are aware of their wounds and looking to addressing healing as soon as possible. It would also be beneficial to anyone that has previous experience with therapy and is not intimidated by the idea of asking for professional help.

It is up to the individual to decide which group they might benefit more from because they each offer different things. It is much more important that the victim is taking steps toward becoming whole again, and either of these methods is a leap in the right direction.

Meditation

We have all seen the way that pop culture represents meditation. There is always a quirky new-age character that meditates, wears only loose-fitting clothing and is probably about to try and sell you essential oils. This characterization is not serious but does some damage to our openness in regard to trying real techniques that have been proven to work. The first question on everyone's mind when meditation is mentioned is what exactly is it?

Meditation is the process of teaching your mind to be calm and therefore exercising a measure of control over your whole emotional state. This is done by creating moments of mindfulness in which your focus is directed to one specific thing. If meditation is practiced with some regularity, it can have a formidable effect on the way that we think.

To meditate in the most effective way, you should be sitting on the floor so that you remain awake throughout the whole session. Your legs should be crossed over one another like we all use to sit in school. Sitting in this manner will allow the rest of your body to relax, which is what we want. Your head should be allowed to be in a comfortable and fixed position, and your eyes should be closed.

Mindfulness Breathing Meditation is one of the more simple exercises, to begin with, and is exactly what it sounds like. You'll need to set aside five minutes a day (use your phone's timer), at first. Find a comfortable place on the floor and close your eyes. Breathe through your nose and concentrate only on that. During this time, you will be focused only on the physical sensation of breathing and the way that it feels to you. It's a physical awareness, only. Forgive yourself if your thoughts begin to wander off, but then just allow yourself to drift back into an awareness of your body. This drifting away in your thoughts and coming back to awareness is the teaching aspect of meditation. You are training your mind to work for you and be calm and at the moment at your command.

It is very much worth looking up more complicated methods of meditation. Increasing the length of time that you're meditating will benefit you in a big way. It takes a varying amount of time for everyone before they begin to see results from this practice.

The most notable of the changes that you will see through using meditation is the drop-in stress levels. We have mentioned in previous chapters that victims of narcissistic abuse have an unfortunate relationship with cortisol, the stress hormone. Those who practice meditation everyday notice a huge drop in stress. Meditation is one of the most effective methods of de-stressing that doesn't involve medicine.

Abuse survivors will have a uniquely good experience with meditation because their most vicious enemy after the relationship, is an ugly internal dialogue. There are so many voices in a victim's head, reminding them of the trauma that they have gone through, and how they do not measure up to their old sense of self. This doubtful inner demon will stick with you through thick and thin (unlike the narcissist), so think of meditation as a way to unglue the stormy self-deprecation from your thoughts. Meditation will teach the individual practicing, to exert anxiety.

The symptoms of stress can act as a plague upon our bodies in general, from irritability to insomnia. So, meditation can also be a step toward physical health. Especially when you take into consideration the amount of damage that these relationships can impart upon our brains. There is almost no drug as effective as meditation.

Meditation also reigns supreme at defeating depression and boosting self-esteem. Practicing meditation is beyond a chemical reaction in the brain; it also responsible for allowing us to be more emotionally healthy. This is because meditation allows the individual to take back their mental autonomy and stops the behaviors that allow us to slip into cycles of negativity. Meditation can prevent us from dwelling on the darkness of our abuse, and keep us focused on our own body, the present moment and logic.

As people of the modern era, our attention span can sometimes take a hit. We have instant access to all sorts of information, and this can overload our ability to sit down and concentrate on one thing. If reading is something that was interesting to you a long time ago, but now you find yourself unable to sit down and enjoy a book, this next benefit is for you. Meditation is shown to have a positive relationship with attention span. The act itself is an exercise in attention, as you will be continuously tempted away from peace by the thoughts zipping through your head. The more you meditate, the more stress-free and attentive to the moment, you will be. This can be put to use in a productive way by meditating before you work.

There is also scientific evidence that shows that daily meditation is able to heighten your mental acuity. This can be especially important to survivors of abuse that drag around in a mental fog. Meditation could be the key to lighting the darkness that seems to hang over the thoughts of a person who has been abused. Meditation can improve your ability to produce, which is great news for those in the workforce who have lost their ability to complete projects.

Meditation also has the surprising effect of allowing us to control other parts of our mind, for example, our pain tolerance. There is evidence to suggest that those who meditate daily do not feel physical pain in the same way as everyone else. Meditation appears to really dampen the effects that pain has on the brain. Meditation is the superfood of the mind.

Abuse can cause so many negative changes both in the body and in mind. Meditation is a counteraction to all most all of these side effects. Stress from the abuse can weigh on the mind and again produce cortisol. This means that sleep takes a direct hit from stress, and lack of sleep means that you feel generally awful and unmotivated. This is another area where meditation can significantly improve an issue and allow those suffering to skip trial and error with medication. Meditating before you sleep will allow your body to calm down and become grounded before you attempt to fall asleep. No more lying in bed for hours, wishing that your thoughts would stop racing because you will be pre-wound-down and ready to drift away.

Meditation also improves the quality of the sleep that you're able to achieve. Many people have an issue with remaining asleep. There is a battle waged between the two sides of consciousness while you sleep and losing that battle could mean that you are going to be waking up several times throughout the night. Interrupted sleep can cause us to feel drowsy and unready for our day in the morning. Meditation is a secret weapon on the side of sleep, in the war for our rest. If you meditate before bed, then you will wake up feeling renewed and ready to start your day. Your mental stamina will benefit from this decision in all the ways that a rested mind is better than an exhausted mind.

Meditation can also assist with memory retention, which is another area that victims of abuse, specifically, tend to suffer from. Cortisol is one of the many chemical changes that the survivors are going to be fighting against, and as we discussed earlier, it has a measured negative effect on the brain. Those looking to combat the symptoms from the over-production of cortisol will greatly benefit from meditation. Improving your memory is just one of the many really beneficial aspects of meditation.

Meditation is overwhelmingly good for us, but why is that? Stress, for humans, is inevitable, and we spend a great deal of time consumed by our own worry and negative expectations. Meditation is just practicing being present in the moment and listening to what the body has to say. There are so many things that tear our attention away from the moment that we are living in, and this is especially true for victims of abuse. Survivors have learned to cope with a life that is near-constant anxiety. There is so much turbulence involved with being close to a narcissist and meditation fights back almost every single long-term symptom of living your life in a hostile environment.

Yoga

Yoga is another alternative form of therapy that may aid in the healing process of those who have been in abusive relationships. Yoga is packed full of both mental and physical benefits, but like meditation, you must practice it daily in order to see benefits from it.

Blood flow can be stimulated in many yoga poses, and that means that both mind and muscles will be running at peak performance. Yoga is also shown to increase the intake of oxygen to the cells, which is also helpful when it comes to protecting and increasing the functionality of the body.

One of the main benefits of exercising after a trauma can be that the heart rate is increased, and the body responds positively to that sort of activity. This can cause the brain to release endorphins that make us feel good. Yoga can also aid in building stamina.

Probably one of the most notable problems that yoga can fix for us is a reduction in cortisol levels. High cortisol levels are a serious issue for those that have survived abusive relationships. Cortisol is responsible or the stress that the victim learns to live with post-breakup. If practiced over the long-term, yoga can significantly reduce our anxiety levels.

Depression is also a common trait that many survivors share. There are so many negative dialogues playing out in the minds of victims, that it is no wonder that many people leave narcissistic relationships with mental health issues. Serotonin is promoted by yoga, and this is another hormone that is responsible for making us feel good.

Yoga also carries many physical benefits like flexibility and muscle tone. Practicing yoga long-term can also help with weight loss. These physical benefits should not be overlooked, because being healthy and feeling good about yourself is one baby step closer to healing from the trauma.

Long-term benefits from yoga can look a little like the long-term benefits from meditation, and there is a reason for that. Yoga is the same practice of being present in the moment and not allowing one's thoughts to run away. The way that stress becomes so prevalent has a lot to do with the way that we are never involved at the moment. Victims of abuse can have a good deal of trouble with worry and anxiety because that was essentially their lifestyle before the relationship ended.

We learned in the previous chapter that being present in the moment can play a huge role in our overall health. It teaches us to focus on one thing, instead of letting our worries consume us before our day even has a chance to begin. Stress has the tendency to cause us to worry about more than what is necessary at any given moment. This can mean that you are eating breakfast in the morning, but in your mind, you're addressing all of the things that you have no means to resolve at the current moment.

By learning to focus our attention on something like breathing or the feeling in our bodies, we allow our mind to escape from the hell that is anxiety. This is another exercise in bringing our attention to one area and is essentially taking both your mind and your body to the gym for fitness.

Yoga allows us to flip a switch in our bodies that allows us to go from systems made to handle stressful situations to the restorative systems that allow us a reprieve from cortisol. We can use yoga to let go of the *fight or flight* stress response so that we exist in a more balanced state.

Yoga is also perfect for allowing us to release physical tension, the kind that we hold in our bodies. Have you ever suddenly become aware of your jaw, only to realize that it's clinched for no reason? The poses in yoga are created to make us aware of the tension in our limbs, and to allow us to release it through changing positions. For victims of abuse, there can be so much build up tension that they are not aware of. Yoga can be more than a mental cure in that way.

Meditation and yoga meet again under the subject of insomnia and sleep quality. The movement of our bodies can allow for unwinding before we drift off to sleep. Yoga can also make us calm before we drift off to slumber, meaning that we are able to fall asleep sooner and stay sleeping throughout the night.

The main concern of yoga and meditation is to foster a peace of mind that might not otherwise be possible in the world that we live in. Victims have different demands on their bodies and are able to improve their state of mind through these activities significantly.

Being a victim of abuse can take a toll on mental clarity and the ability to rely on your own logic. Survivors have a long road ahead of them because they must relearn to trust themselves, but practices such as these make it a lot easier to find the motivation for the journey. Living with someone who plays mind games with you and continually causes you to doubt your own perception of reality can be disheartening, and there are so many aftershocks from the abuse that can be just as painful. It is in this way that we come to understand the real benefits of yoga.

Yoga is not only an exercise that can be used to better your body, but there is also an aspect of philosophy that guides the practice. There are beliefs that are tangled up in the movements, that allow a person to really reflect on who they are and their place in the universe. Should you do your best to throw yourself into the teachings of yoga, you have the ability to turn your way of life around completely. The philosophy asserts that we are all perfect and a reflection of divinity. Slowly bit by bit, yoga teaches us that we are much more than we previously thought. Victims of abuse have been beaten down with such fury, that they are effectively pieces of a person. With exercises like meditation and yoga, you will be heading down a path of restoration.

Balancing Your Chakras

According to ancient eastern spirituality, our bodies are made up of energy that is vibrating and flowing through us at different frequencies. This energy is concentrated into seven points, directly down the center of the body (ending right before our legs). These balls of energy respond to events in our lives and other stimuli, and these effects can profoundly change the way that the whole body as a system, functions. Whenever someone is experiencing an ailment, spiritual leaders will assess that they are living with an imbalance in the energy flow of the chakra that corresponds with the ailment.

For example, should an individual notice that their kidney has started hurting them, the answer to that would be that the sacral chakra is blocked. To allow the flow of energy to resume, the person would need to take action. Chakras are balanced by doing spiritual exercise, chanting, specific yoga poses, or even color therapy.

Every chakra comes equipped with associated color and guttural sound, and these two things can make it easier to visualize. Visualization is a method repair for chakras that are blocked or otherwise unable to perform. You may use the color, vibration, and location to affect change in the desired way.

Chakras may be damaged by major life events, the food that we eat, and even potentially our own negative mindset. This means that victims of abuse could carry a lot of their damage in a spiritual way.

Spirituality has been a reflection of how the whole civilizations of people view their health and body for as long as mankind has been around. These ideas have been passed down for so long, with millions of people invested in their ethereal welfare. These ideas still hold value today, all over the world. It is a fascinating subject that consumes so many of us, with many principals that carry over into modern medicine. Meditation, yoga, and chakra work are all tools used in an attempt to better our health and happiness. Exploring your spirituality can be a very valuable way for an individual to bring about healing within themselves because, at the very least, these exercises can make you more aware of your own body.

Root Chakra: Muladhara is the given name of the root chakra, and its color is a brilliant ruby red. In most texts, it will be represented by a lotus blossom. "LAM" is the sound associated with this chakra. Picture yourself seated with your legs crossed. This chakra is at the bottom-most area of your body. It resides around the base of the spine and travels a path along the perineum, the first three vertebrae of the spine and the pelvic plexus. This chakra is associated with our most instinctual nature and the feelings of security, in short, it is responsive to the most basic needs for our survival. The root chakra is also associated with the fight or flight response. Should you find yourself flying into a rage, or rushing too quickly to any emotion, this chakra is probably off balance according to the spiritual study. It is the foundation upon which all of our other chakras rest, and therefore must be maintained.

An imbalance in this chakra will result in the individual feeling uneasy, greedy, or overly negative. To balance the root chakra, it is best to use meditation. You may sit with your legs crossed and your back straight. Focus your attention on the area of your physical body, where you are touching the ground with your spine. Try to envision this chakra, and silently focus on your connection with the earth. You may also focus on your nose because this chakra is also associated with the sense of smell. Basic flow yoga or exercise of any fashion will also allow you to center yourself in regard to this chakra.

Sacral Chakra: This chakra is also known by Svadhishthana and is associated with a bright orange hue. On your body, the sacral chakra is located about three inches below your navel.

This chakra is the embodiment of our creativity, sexuality, emotional connections to others, and pleasure. Water is another popular way to symbolize this chakra, and that has a lot to do with the flow of energy through you. Imagery may also include the moon and a flower-like circle.

Abuse victims will have the most imbalance in this chakra, as it is very sensitive to controlling behavior. Imbalance will look like codependency, loss of libido, feeling empty, or being impulsive and under the control of your emotions. Someone that has been in close contact with a narcissist, especially if the narcissist was/is a romantic partner, will have issues with intimacy. Eastern spiritualism purports that you may be able to adjust some of these problems by balancing this chakra.

To realign the sacral chakra tantric yoga can be a wonderful tool. The warrior pose is said to carry a lot of power in this area. Meditation is also a useful tool in repairing the blockage. Think of the behavior that you wish to change and meditate while thinking about the opposite of the behavior. If you're feeling numb and empty, then your meditation should be focused on passion. It helps visualize the physical location and color of the chakra while you're doing this.

You may also be able to re-establish the flow of this chakra by finding a new hobby or activity of interest. This should work to reignite the passion and intensity that is the lifeblood of this chakra. It is also important that you are able to confront and overcome the experience that is serving as a blockage. You can do this by trying to understand your own personal trauma and working not to identify yourself with the pain. Should you continue to meditate and detach yourself from your past injuries or mistakes, then you will eventually transcend the pain that these actions or events have caused you.

Solar Plexus Chakra: This chakra goes by the name Manipura, and you will see it associated with the color yellow. This chakra is symbolized by a ten-petal golden lotus flower. You will often see this chakra represented with fire. This is also a very important chakra for abuse victims because it is mostly associated with self-confidence and the power that you have to change your own life. This chakra is flowing as it should when you have a high opinion of yourself and are able to recognize your worth. This chakra may also be tied to your digestion and stamina, meaning if there is an issue with this chakra, then it will be sometimes be felt in your stomach, or your intestines.

Manipura is at the very center of our seated body, from the solar plexus to our breast. The location means that this chakra may also be affected by what we eat and how we choose to nourish our bodies. Our ego can also cause issues in relation to this chakra.

Victims of abuse certainly have some issues with this chakra in particular, because in a narcissistic relationship, self-esteem is the first casualty. Luckily this chakra is not a difficult one to balance. Breathing meditations can significantly assist you in tuning into this chakra. There is a meditation called "Breath of Fire," that is specifically focused on the repair of this chakra. Eating food that is not damaging to the body is another beautiful way to win favor with this particular chakra, as well as taking the time to dress in a manner that we feel confident. This sentiment is not in relation to price, so much as wearing the things that we love. You may also cure this chakra by focusing on the color yellow, look for yellow in the sunset, in flowers and in the pollen on your car in the morning. Positive affirmations that reaffirm your self-esteem are also imperative to balancing this chakra.

Heart Chakra: The Heart Chakra is also known as Anahata and is represented by a beautiful emerald green (and occasionally pink). The heart chakra is misleading in its name because it is located at the bottom of the chest. The imagery used to symbolize this chakra is a star made of two overlapping triangles. The element of air will also be used when balancing this chakra.

The color representations of the chakras are said to correspond with the hue that is emitted from the point of energy on our bodies. This chakra has two because it is said to turn a light rose when the energy is vibrating at a higher frequency. This strong connection to color may be observed throughout the practice of observing and healing chakras. This is also why just focusing on the color that is associated with the chakra, can do a lot in the way of freeing that energy point from the blockage.

Anahata is our relationship chakra, and it is relevant to every stage of our associations. This chakra is important for love, beauty, empathy, acceptance, transformation, grieving, and most importantly, forgiveness. Balancing this chakra can provide another very useful resource for those that have been victims of narcissistic relationships. Survivors may work with the chakra to enable them to let go of some of the rages that victims hold for their abusers. This is not a service to the guilty party in the relationship, but a way the free the victim from the psychological effects of bitterness. This chakra has the potential to lighten the burden of trauma felt by those that have been exposed to prolonged abuse.

Many symptoms suggest that this chakra is blocked, including but not limited to a physical ache in the lower middle portion of the chest. Feelings of bitterness, loneliness/isolation, envy, and the feeling that you're tightly holding a grudge, may all be signs that this chakra is unbalanced.

The accouterments that go along with the opening of Anahata have a tendency to reflect the chakra's relationship to the color's green and pink. Many practitioners recommend the use of both green and pink candles along with jade and rose quartz. Meditation is also a preferred method for opening up this chakra, but there are some really simple steps to take that ensure you are caring for the balance of Anahata.

Practice examining old wounds and allowing yourself to forgive the people that have injured you in the past. It will be difficult to facilitate the flow if the reason that the chakra is blocked is unknown. Allow yourself to sit in a comfortable position and take deep breaths, visualize the warmth in your heart growing as you inhale. Focus on the color green and all of the natural beauty that accompanies it.

Throat Chakra: Vishudda is the Sanskrit name for this chakra, which focuses primarily on communication. Sound and a baby blue hue represent the throat chakra. This chakra is associated with communication of all types, including expression through creation and nonverbal.

When this chakra is imbalanced, it can manifest in many different ways, including physical ailments with the throat. The issue that you will see most closely assigned to this chakra is the feeling that you're aren't being understood when you attempt to communicate with others. If you have ever tried to explain something to someone and they just will not take you seriously, or they misinterpret your statements, then that could be a sign that either you or the person that you're speaking to have a blocked throat chakra. The throat chakra is also considered the energy center of the body, so if you are ever feeling creatively blocked or lazy, then this chakra could also potentially be to blame

The throat chakra can specifically affect victims of abuse because of its relationship with fear. More signs that there may potential blockage include social anxiety or panic that is triggered by thoughts of telling the truth about something. With the amount of criticism that victims of narcissistic abuse have faced, it is no surprise that they may deal with hesitation in speaking about the experience with therapists or love ones. There may just be fear in general regarding telling others their side of a story.

There are two theories when it comes to unblocking or balancing chakras. There are some that believe that there is no such thing as a chakra being too open and there is no merit to the concept of "balancing," but rather that any issues with chakras may be addressed by opening the chakra back up. The other side of the coin consists of those who think that there is such a thing as a charka being "too open" and those people claim that when the throat chakra is too open, the individual has no control over what they say. The idea from these specialists is that the chakra needs to be ajar, or the verbal filter will go missing, and the person will just say anything that pops into their mind.

The throat chakra may be balanced in a number of ways, including all the old favorites like meditation, yoga, and visualization. There are also some fun new ways to balance this chakra, and the easiest of those would be singing. Sing or hum along whenever you get the chance, this chakra loves sound and vibration. The throat chakra may also be addressed by journaling your feelings or recording them via the voice recorder on your phone. You will see the phrase "speak your truth" associated with this chakra quite a lot.

Food also plays a large role in the health of the throat chakra and eating a diet that features fruit heavily, will do a good deal for both your energy and your body. Drinking a lot of water will also be of value for insuring the health of Vishudda.

The Third Eye Chakra: The third eye chakra is also referred to as Ajna and is usually represented with a glowing purple or blue tone. It is located between the eyes and is known as the seat of intuition in the body. The third eye chakra is shrouded in lore and mystery, and for a good reason. It is the connection of the physical body to other states of consciousness through the eyes. Ajna's element is perception itself.

There is a lot going on with the third eye chakra, as it can allow us to subconsciously comprehend truths that we otherwise have no knowledge of in the physical world. This chakra also has close ties to wisdom, sleep/melatonin, and inspiration. Ajna is also associated with spirituality, and if it is blocked, then there is a hopeless feeling of disconnect with the universe. Intuition may be vastly improved by opening this chakra, but as mentioned before, there are those who think that the chakras can become too open. If Ajna is opened too far and the rest of the body is out of sync, it can mean that the affected individual is swept away in a world of daydreaming and out of touch with reality. Physical symptoms that this chakra is closed may include chronic headaches and sinus pain. This chakra may also cause pain within the eyes.

This chakra may prove to be an issue for victims of narcissistic abuse in many ways, being that large periods of change have the potential to really mess up the alignment of Ajna. Having your reality or interest challenged will also cause blockage, and we know abusers thrive on being able to reroute the victim's thoughts.

To align this chakra, it is best to practice seeing without one's eyes. Sit or lay in a black room and visualize a white glowing light in the area where this chakra would be located (between the eyes). Dark chocolate is a fun way to balance this chakra, along with eating foods that are a rich purple color.

The Crown Chakra: The crown chakra is also known as Sahasrara, and it is located at the very top of the head. It is represented by a thousand petal lotus flower and is represented by a fuchsia color. Imagine that the top of the head is the center of the lotus blossom, and the petals extend out and away from us. This chakra is our connection to the universe and everything that is beyond us and divine.

Sahasrara, if opened, may act as another booster to our intuition. This chakra is closely tied with our brains, and it can be a gateway to wisdom and peace. If you are experiencing any confusion about the next path to take, this chakra can be a valuable asset in deciphering your own goals.

This is another chakra that is easy to relate to the struggles of abuse victims because it is associated with your inner peace. Sahasrara is also the bringer of beauty and has a lot to do with general motivation. Symptoms that this chakra is blocked are depression, self-destruction, pessimism, headaches, and chronic exhaustion. There are many more physical and psychological issues that can occur when we have a closed-off crown chakra.

When those we care about mock the things that we are interested in, this chakra takes a huge hit. This chakra may also be thrown out of alignment when we disbelieve or distrust our connection to the divine. Whatever divine means to the individual is open to their own interpretation, but a disconnect will cause the individual to feel apathetic. Those we were close to, speaking ill of us or taking actions that are a detriment to our growth may also cause stagnation within this chakra.

All of the usual suspects have shown up to the healing party for this chakra: meditation, visualization, yoga, and color therapy. You may also spend time trying to participate in activities that make you feel creative or inspire you. Music, art, and culture may all be consumed in an effort to open this chakra back up. Silence may also be just the medicine that you need for this chakra, and sitting in silence will allow you to still your thoughts and open this chakra. Open-mindedness will also aid in both this chakram and your development as a person. Allow yourself to look at things from other perspectives, because that is the lifeblood of wisdom, consider everything.

Clear quartz can be used to unblock this chakra. Eat some foods that share their color with this chakra—red grapes can be a great place to start. Affirmations can also be used to aid in the balancing of this chakra, phrases such as "I am connected." This chakra is all about our ties to the universe, and that is why it holds such an important place on our bodies.

Neuro-Linguistic Programming (NLP)

Abuse survivors have a lot of internal dialogue that is informing negative and self-destructive behaviors. Trauma has the tendency to manifest a dramatic change in the way that people think. Every method of therapy that we look at is a measure to turn back the clock of the detrimental changes and turn the mind into a well-oiled machine that is even more effective than it was before the abuse. NLP or **Neuro-Linguistic Programming** is a method of changing one's behavior by using other individuals as a model.

NLP also suggests that our internal dialogue causes most of the issues that we have with your own actions. This form of therapy seeks to assess the underlying fear that is causing the physical reaction within us, so that it may be addressed directly. NLP also asserts that practicing its techniques will put the individual more in touch with their inner world, and allow them to affect the changes that they would like to see in their own thought process. Neuro-Linguistic Programming has also shown the potential to ease symptoms in those with PTSD from life-changing trauma.

When we think of communication, we think of language. This is the way that the whole world uses speech as an exchange of information. Practitioners of NLP work through a different means of communication, namely body language, eye moment, and other subtle physical nuances. They also believe that our inner system of communication is comprised of images, feelings, and sounds. This means that once you're able to speak the language of your body, you will be able to understand the behavior that could have appeared as foreign to you before.

The four pillars of NLP are rapport through sensory acuity, outcome thinking, sensory awareness, and behavioral flexibility. Rapport states that by understanding the way that others communicate, one may mimic this communication to create a bond of trust with the individual quickly. Outcome thinking involves thinking about the thing that you wish to achieve instead of allowing the negative words in your head to guide you into hesitation. Sensory awareness is the principal that your senses can inform you about the world more fully when you are paying close attention to them. Behavioral flexibility is the idea that the most successful participants with NLP are able to change behaviors that do not work for them anymore. This is an important quality to have if you aim to benefit from NLP because it is all about changing your behaviors until you're able to find something that works.

NLP recognizes the way that when we observe something in the outside world, we run said thing through the different elements of our perception. Our mind has a way of filtering the information that we observe through our culture, beliefs, language, values, memories, and decisions. The product of viewing the thing through our lens is called our **internal representation.** We can use the internal representation to affect the changes in our behavior. Psychologists have long ago proved that stimuli have a relationship to automatic behavior and NLP ventures that successful behaviors are also automated. If we are able to change our internal representation when presented with stimuli, that means that we can author our own successful behavior patterns.

NLP also asserts that if we can learn about the internal representations of people that we view to be our own actualized ideas, then we can also use those individuals to rewrite our own internal representations to be successful.

The human mind is like a computer, and the internal representation coupled with the state of mind and physical being produces a behavior. The more knowledge that we have about our thought process, the more we are the masters of our behavior. According to NLP, have a different perspective on our issues is the solution to them. Those closer we come to determining our actual issues, or the problems behind our fear or anger, the closer we are to being able to reprogram that behavior within ourselves.

It is also worth noting that NLP recognizes that our brains do not process negative things in a direct way, so while this school of thought is all about positive affirmations, you must avoid telling your mind not to do something. If someone were to hand you a closed box and ask you not to look inside, they have created a whole thought scenario (internal representation) in your head, in which you open the box. Like teenagers, our minds are keen on following requests that begin with "do not do this."

NLP can be a very useful tool for those that want to author their own mental health. It serves to strengthen the communication that one has with their own body for the good of the mind. There are so many tools that go along with recognizing, deconstructing, and rewriting your own behavior. Even a basic understanding of NLP could enable the victim of abuse to change the language that they use to address their issues in their own minds.

Cognitive Processing Therapy (CPT)

Cognitive Processing Therapy (or CPT) is used as a resource for those who have endured traumatic events and can be especially helpful for those with PTSD. This form of therapy is for those who have been trapped by their own understanding of their trauma. Abuse victims may suffer from mental health that is frozen in time, as they struggle to go about their day-to-day life healthily and productively.

CBT is typically a twelve-session course that is designed to change the way that the individual processes trauma. Trauma has the ability to rock the very foundation of our mental health. It can change everything about us from the way that we relate to other people to our feelings of safety and security in any given environment. PTSD has the ability to cause the sufferers to fear for their lives in situations where that fear is not helpful. It is believed that trauma can cause a breakup of our preexisting perceptions, and this can manifest as the victim feeling "stuck."

By writing and communicating with the therapist, the patient learns techniques to rewire their thinking when it comes to how they receive information. This therapy seeks to teach the patient to look at the events from a different perspective, as a means to break the cycle of feeling like they are trapped.

CPT is unique because the patient is allowed to take on a more active role in his or her recovery. The therapist will eventually put the sessions in the hands of the patient and act more as a guide. There is a lot of writing in this method of therapy. It is also unique because of how quickly patients are able to see results.

The first goal of CPT is to help the patient reflect upon the pain that they have encountered. For victims of narcissistic abuse, this would mean focusing on the effect of the abuse that they have suffered. The patient would also be challenged to think critically about the impact of the trauma on their lives now, and to change the way that they interact with these changes. Avoidance can be extremely tempting when it comes to trauma, but this sort of reaction is counterproductive. The patient is asked to work on the amount of times that they react to the pain with numbness and avoiding behaviors.

The therapist's next step is to assist the patient in redefining the way that they think about their trauma. The patient will learn to re-work the story of their trauma in their head, from the point of view that they are better able to understand and live with. This means viewing negative events from a perspective that is not just "all people are evil." The patient is taught to challenge the negative dialogue in their own head, that is causing them to feel trapped.

The last and final goal of this therapy is to help the patient recover from the symptoms of their abuse. This means that they are able to move forward with their mental health journey and lessen the feelings of anxiety, rage, shame, and guilt. All of these things combined may give the patient back their sense of self because they will no longer just be reacting to the threatening things in their lives.

In CPT, the patient's goal is to become more literate in their own feelings and thoughts, especially the things that are triggering for them. **Stuck Points** are developed as a reaction to PTSD. They are thought that make it difficult for the patient to recover. The patient will learn to identify these stuck points and critically analyze the thinking that causes them.

The patient will learn to redirect the thoughts that make up stuck points so that they are able to overcome them. Eventually, the patient will address the change in their own belief system in relation to the trauma and the world around them.

Emotional Freedom Technique

The Emotional Freedom Technique (or EFT) is a form of acupuncture that involves tapping. EFT is focused on healing the emotional wounds left from abuse and trauma. This is a physical form of therapy that revolves around getting to know your own body and the energy that your emotions are responsible for producing. By exploring the emotions that we feel, and really allowing ourselves to understand them, we are able to begin the healing process.

Victims of narcissistic abuse are plagued with a lot of emotional uncertainty. The best tools to use to overcome the distress that builds up in our bodies means that we must confront even the most negative aspects of the pain that we feel. We often attempt to recoil from pain because that is much simpler than allowing it to tear us down, but what if we were able to meet these feelings and conquer them? This would change the way that we address trauma all together and could be very beneficial to those that learn how.

Survivors may suffer from anxiety and rage, as well as frequent thoughts of suicide. Long-term abuse can also change the way that we perceive the world. Feelings of helplessness and shame are common in the lives of those that have lived through such toxic relationships. There are also reoccurring thoughts that the victim somehow deserves all of the abuser's actions toward them. Abuse may also cause the victim to become socially withdrawn and very skeptical of others. Trauma can create a feeling that the suffering party will never be safe, and this extends to every environment. Just going to work or going out with friends can become a terrifying reminder that it seems like they are never going to free from their mental shackles. Hopelessness becomes a way of life for anyone that has dealt with abuse for any extended period of time. The goal of the Emotional Freedom technique is to address both of the physical and emotional symptoms of pain.

This healing technique is practiced by repeating positive affirmations while tapping on the energy centers on your body. Practitioners of EFT believe that the body is made of this energy, and it flows through us along pathways called **meridians**. In the same way that we discussed with chakras, when these energy pathways become blocked, then we may experience both physical and emotional issues. All acupuncture works with the same philosophy about the body, and whether you are being stuck with needles or you're tapping on your skin, those energy centers are the points that are being engaged.

The Emotional Freedom Technique is a new age blending of ideas that come from both spiritualism, neuro-linguistic programming and psychology, and it works very well for deleting negative feelings from the body. One of the exercises consists of identifying something that the subject is afraid of and allowing them to rate the fear on a scale from one to ten. The subject is then guided to tap the energy centers while speaking the fear aloud. Eventually, if all goes as it is supposed to, the level at which the subject has rated the fear will begin to fall back to zero.

Tapping has also been proven to dramatically lessen anxiety at the moment by using the same method mentioned above. We discussed the amygdala in a previous chapter, and it is to blame for the warm rush of adrenaline that we feel right before a panic attack. Tapping has the ability to counteract these effects by sending a soothing signal to the amygdala. With so many positive results already on the books, EFT makes a wonderful tool to add to your healing arsenal.

Mirror Work

Each form of therapy or healing technique that we have learned about so far serves a different purpose along the healing journey. Mirror work is no different and is aimed toward teaching a measure of self-love. An individual who has been exposed to prolonged abuse is obviously in need of a self-esteem boost, but of course, there is more to it than that. Learning to love yourself again is vital to ensuring that you're able to move forward from the darkness of your past. It is also a means by which to ensure that victims do not ever find themselves in the position of being narcissistic supply ever again.

Mirror work is about developing a new relationship with yourself, via speaking to the mirror as you would a loved one. The mirror is used to connect with the deepest part of your subconscious, which is longing for affection. Louise Hay made mirror work famous with her book of the same name, and from the time that she introduced the public to this valuable technique, people have been raving about the impressive results. Hay claimed that speaking to the mirror was an effort to speak to your inner child.

This technique is about taking the time to commune with oneself. It rejects the commonplace practice of passing a mirror and breathing a heavy sigh about the parts of ourselves that we dislike. Mirror work focuses on biting off as little or as much as you can each day, slowly learning to love and forgive yourself through thoughtful communication. This method has the ability to sit us down opposite of someone with familiar eyes that gaze at us as we try to untangle the damage, we've allowed to taint the way that we see ourselves.

Art Therapy

Mankind has been expressing itself with art from its conception, and our interest in creativity is a sign that our brains function at a higher cognitive capacity than any of our other animal neighbors. Art is an abstract means of reflection upon ourselves and the world around us. Creativity is one of many ways that we showcase the self-awareness that separates us from the rest of cognizant life.

Art therapy is exactly what it sounds like, using art as a method for looking at the trauma or pain that an individual is experiencing. Trained psychologists guide their patients to create, and in this process, every choice is significant. With this form of therapy, the level of artistic expertise is not a factor. Art therapy may be used to help patients who haven't held a marker since grade school because the focus is the emotion that is driving the expression.

This method of therapy works so well because the psychologist is using art as a medium by which to speak to their client's true emotions. The patient is also using the projects as a release for a lot of the intense feelings (rage, sadness, fear) that they have been allowing to build up inside of them.

The therapist facilitates the work by allowing the patient to create their piece and then using the art as a discussion tool. The therapist will ask questions about creative choices that were made within the piece and how they correspond to the issues that the patient is having. Therapists are not expected to have a ledger of the symbology that a client has chosen, used to dissect the meaning of the image. Instead, this exchange is the patient abstractly expressing themselves and then using a dialogue with a trained professional in order to come to some sort of understanding about the message of the piece.

Art therapy also creates a physical token by which to measure and celebrate the progress that the patient is making. There are many different exercises that allow patients to explore their inner psyche through creativity. Art therapy requires courage on behalf of the patient because they are bearing their souls. This practice can also have a profoundly positive effect on those looking to chase away their inner demons.

Personal growth is not a quantitative study, and there are so many beautiful things that you may choose to do in order to progress along your healing journey. The most important thing to take away is that you are in control of your process and your own timeline. Even the abuse is just another chapter in a grand book that you are writing as you venture down the path of life. The pain of transformation is the most intimate way in which we get to know ourselves. Trauma is a catalyst to explore the darker areas of our own nature, so that we may understand and forgive ourselves for being human. Trauma is not the end of the road, but rather it may act as a building block for our own evolution.

CHAPTER 6

Learning to Love Again

Trauma, the word is profound and dangerous. It carries meanings that many of us can't fathom, and it invokes a sort of fear response in us. There are flashes of people crying on the floor, blankly staring at themselves in the mirror and looking pensively at the phone in front of them. We know that damage is inherent in life, and there is nothing that we can do to avoid every negative thing. Still, many of us have never thought that we would ever think of ourselves as a "victim" until we did.

As humans, we are both natures' most resilient and self-aware creatures. This cognition comes at a jarring price, as carry our pain on our shoulders for years. Significant trauma can cause an echo that spans decades, as we struggle to make sense of the things that we have experienced. There are those among us that live in utter agony, trying their best to understand the piece of themselves that was taken from them.

Abuse is a funny thing; for that reason, it sometimes takes an outsider to inform us that anything is out of the ordinary, in the first place. Most of us are altruistic creatures by nature and will take on any emotional burden if it means that we are able to spare our partners from feeling the way that we do.

Narcissists prey on those around us that make a mission of understanding and helping others. They feast on the affection that is freely given to them by empaths and others who strive only to make others happy. Abusers are so detrimental to our nature because they reciprocate none of the efforts that their partners make and instead tear away at the victim's sense of self. Narcissists go around communicating with the world like they aren't hunting for their next meal. They shuffle among us in disguise, hiding the void that is their nature.

Those who don't understand will say time and time again, that they would never allow themselves to fall victim to the charm of the hunter. They are ignorant of the fact that we were made to be the most perfect prey because most people only want to save the lost soul.

When another person comes to you, a vision of the partner that you have created in your head, you will do almost anything to ensure that they see you. This is the trap because everything they have told you is fake. The giant lies, meant to catch you like a fly in their web. They somehow like all the same music that you do, all of the same things are important to them. At first, they fit into your life like a missing puzzle piece. They have observed you and decided that you should be their supply.

They come off as complicated and different from anyone you have ever met. Instead of a red flag, you see their strangeness as refreshing. You slowly let them, and you make memories that feel like an ethereal realization of all the rom-com fantasies in your head. This was meant to be, and no one will be able to tell you otherwise. Except everyone tells you otherwise, friends and family see it coming long before you do. They only say these things because they don't understand, and that is the thought that you find yourself thinking more and more.

Then the tears begin, they've said something that no one else has ever said to you in a fight. They have seen you bear your soul, and they used these opportunities to find the weak spot. They know exactly how to cause you pain. They exactly where to apply the pressure. The misery that you feel in this moment is terrifying, and your heart is broken.

They use this as a chance to gloat because look at how much they mean to you! The abuser is secretly celebratory because this was just an exercise in their power. They are now going to shower you with affection and attention. The abuser will apologize for being vicious and sound, so sure of the course of action that they need to take to turn their behavior around. So many days of doubt turn into days of hope because the person that you fell in love with is still in there. They are not the monster that they accidentally showed to you that day, they are still the love of your life.

The love of your life has been acting weird lately. They hid their phone whenever you walk by. Instead of spending time with you, they will isolate themselves in another room and talk to other people across the internet. They challenge every word that you say to them. They push you into walls, bragging that at least they don't hit you.

The love of your life has become hostile toward you, and you are anxious all of the time now. They are angry with your family and friends for warning you against them. They are annoyed by driving you to work, after asking you to sell your car. When you try to speak to them, they turn your words against you like you're stupid and crazy. They shove you, break your things, and try to turn everyone else against you.

You threaten to leave, and they threaten to kill themselves. How could you do this to them when they needed you the most? You must have never really loved them, the abuser screams, you are only capable of loving yourself. You give up;

you try to comfort them. You're pretty sure that they're going to kill you, you just don't know when.

Life passes before your eyes. Your family and friends are happily going about their days with peace of mind and people that love them. You are alone, crying every night on the bathroom floor. Even the days that start out alright end with you being kicked out of a pulled-over car on the highway or chasing your partner down the street in a desperate effort to keep them from causing a giant scene and getting arrested. They blame you for the way that their life has turned out. You want it all to be over.

Then one day it happens...they have kept you awake all night, banging on the walls and screaming. You beg them to stop, and they accidentally demand that you leave right this moment. You know they don't mean it, and they just want to gut you emotionally, but you may never get another chance so you pack up everything that will fit into a couple of trash bags. You call your best friend to pick you up, and you run.

You used to be one whole person, but now you are pieces of a person plopped right back down in the normal. Of course, the ex is calling you over and over, but you have no idea what to do other than to exist. You are in shock, going out to eat again with all of your friends and knowing that you don't have the words to describe the horror that you have endured. You stare blankly at your food, as they run over memory after memory and laugh. They are so glad to have you back, and you're so thankful to be back, but they will never know about the mess inside of you.

This is a struggle that millions of people go through every year. If you have found this book because you have been through this yourself, first of all, congratulations. The hardest part is over. Escaping whatever your version of hell looked like, is one of the most trying things that anyone can go through. You likely feel like an alien that has been dropped into the human world, and you should know that it is absolutely normal. This is going to take so much time to beat, and the process of healing is going to change you in ways that you'd never guessed.

The title of the chapter is "Learning to Love Again," so how do you even do that? Well, you don't, yet. You can't, yet. Narcissistic relationships tear the victim down from the inside out, and as we have read earlier in the book, it may even cause chemical changes in the brain. You must untangle all of the damaged circuits and relearn yourself completely.

First and foremost, you must never speak to the abuser again. If you already have, forgive yourself and then change your number. The first act of love and repair that you must show yourself is to cut ties with the enemy of your mental health, the narcissist. He or she will never change, and there is nothing you can or should do or them. You are not responsible for the abuser, and everything they say about being hurt is a lie.

Time is the healing hand of nature, and as the hours slip into days, and the days, to years, you will notice something magical. The squeezing claw of the abuser wrapped around your heart? You will feel it less and less every single day. Some days you're forlorn and sobbing, you will never forget this pain. With time, your wounds will fuse together more and more.

Time alone is not enough, though. The victim must take an active role in the recovery process. Use therapy, exercise, acupuncture, or anything, but eventually, you will need to tend to the gaps in your spirit. Fresh out of these relationships, you will not love yourself or even know who you are anymore. Narcissists have the tendency to strip away your sense of self until there is nothing left but a mirror for them to stare at.

All of the healing techniques have one thing in common, and that is that they all demand that you get to know yourself and where the negative feelings come from. Learn to see yourself in the way that the world sees you again. Do the things that allow you to express yourself like music, writing, art, dance, singing, yodeling, etc. Whatever brings you closer to your own soul, you must do that.

I know this is a cliché, but it is a cliché for a reason; you have to learn to love yourself before you allow yourself to love anyone else. Do not rush into another relationship before you understand your trauma. You must address issues with self-destruction and codependency before you attempt to attach yourself to another person.

What would happen if you do not wait before starting a new relationship? Long-term abuse can cause something called C-PTSD (the "C" stands for complex), which is an anxiety disorder that grows its legs from the victim's feeling of being trapped. This disorder will go away when you allow yourself time to heal, but until then, it will cause intense emotional flashbacks to the abuse.

Your super-ego is going to be simultaneously raining criticism down upon you because it has been damaged by the words and actions of your partner. If you're lucky, and you choose someone who isn't a narcissist, then you're going to have a lot of unresolved self-esteem issues that your current partner is going to be paying the price for. The victim is also going to be plagued by mood swings because of the confused state of their emotions and their perception of reality. When you've been gaslighted for an extended period of time, it breaks down your confidence in your own judgment. All of these issues can also serve to make you very untrusting of your new non-narcissist partner.

If you're terribly unlucky, then you have blindly stumbled into the arms of another narcissist, and this is also bad news. Your messy emotional state will make you easy prey, and they have no issues with using your past pain against you all over again.

For all of these reasons, the first person that an abuse victim needs to learn to love is themselves. Abuse victims must take the time to confront the anxiety and their cracked super-ego and sense of self. This is the process of turning from victim to survivor, and if nothing is learned from this experience, then the pain was all for naught. Do whatever it is that you need to do, to really examine these old wounds. Therapists are the best place to start after an experience like this, but healing can be achieved even on one's own.

None of this is to say that you are doomed to be alone forever, but healing comes first. You will know when you are in the position to begin dating again because life will no longer seem like a never-ending chore that you need to complete. You are ready for love again when your passion has returned. When your inner critic has shut up and is letting you get through the day without calling you trash.

Learning to love again also means being watchful and keeping yourself safe from the abuse that you have been set free from. Those that have already been exposed to a narcissist have a unique perspective when it comes to sniffing out the signs. When you and your body are armed and ready to get back on the horse, use your critical thinking skills, and separate your honey-moon-period emotions from the equation for a moment. You're still allowed to enjoy other people but use your past experience to sus out a pretender.

Should you become interested in a new person who seems to immediately morph into the person that you have always wanted, be wary. If the new apple of your eye has a horrible past and is coming to you as a self-proclaimed hero rising from the dust of their own trauma, be wary. Watch for those that take on all of your interests and values. Watch the way they speak about their exes. This is the knowledge that you earned with blood, sweat, and especially tears, so it is your responsibility to put it to use. Watch for charisma, charm, and the "people either love me or hate me" phrase. Remember the love-bombing and the overzealous romantic gestures in the beginning. If the new interest immediately makes statements about no one else understanding them like you, analyze their actions.

In a previous chapter, we discussed the way that the body sometimes understands that things are off before we do, ourselves. Ask your body if the new person of interest is safe, or just listen to the things that your body is already telling you. Butterflies are fun, nervous, and bubbly. Should you feel a wash of uneasiness in the presence of the person, then read into it. Have you ever been minding your own business, and suddenly you are just inundated with the feeling of being watched? That is the body's same alarm system going off for another reason, but it's the same feeling.

Practice can also be a vital tool when you feel that you're ready to entertain the idea of dating again. There are so many sources that like to blame computers and digital communication in the modern era, for all of our societal issues. This is a decidedly good thing about the Internet, you can practice dating from the comfort and safety of your own home. When the time is right, download a dating app or join a website and jump right in. Abuse victims have been so far removed from all the wonder of awkward small talk that goes along with meeting new people. There is no obligation to plan a date or speak to people who are being pushy, but it can be a good exercise to put the very tip of your toe in the door and chat with new people. It is noncommittal, and you may end a conversation at any time, and this way, you are in control.

During the new search, it is a good idea to clear time for a hobby that you love. Do something that keeps self-love on the front burner of your mind. Exercise or creative activity will work for this purpose. You have ideally done a lot of work on your mind already, but this will just serve as a reinforcement. It's not only a conversation starter, but it ensures that you are coming from a positive and healthier place. It is just an insurance policy, so that lowered self-esteem is not the one making the mate selection.

Trust is going to be an obstacle for you on this new journey. You have only just learned how to trust yourself again, so how do you prepare to trust a whole new man or woman? This must be said, do not try to force trust for someone new just because you know that you have an issue with anxiety. Take your time! Trust will develop naturally, and if you have otherwise vetted someone new, then they must be worth the wait. You may even find it necessary to explain the situation, as you would end up having the conversation eventually anyway. Get to really know the new potential partner before you decide to make them anything beyond a friend. Bring them around your friends and family and see how well this person interacts. Ask them about their past relationships. Do any and everything that you need to, in order to feel secure. You have the right to be comfortable. If the new interest is showing any signs of being abusive, conjure up the memories of your last relationship to ease any guilt you might feel about letting them go, and cut them off.

The healing process is all about taking your place in your own heart, as number one. Once you have experienced abuse, you know all too well what trauma looks like. You know every attractive detail of trauma's face. In honor of yourself, respect your memories and never let a narcissist enter your headspace again. Love and healing are a transient part of life, and in time you will be whole. These memories will physically echo through your body as you recoil at the thought of the abuser's face and that same face will eventually fade into the ether as a harsh lesson from your past. Your damaging personal history is the fire that forges the person you will become. Every shadow is cast with a light, and sometimes the light is the wisdom and depth that you obtain from overcoming something that was meant to take you down. You will always carry a few dings in the paint from your past but wear your scars with pride because you earned them in battle.

CONCLUSION

Thank you for making it through to the end of *Narcissistic Partner Abuse: A Healing Guide to Overcoming the Abuse of a Narcissist and Find Yourself*. Narcissist abuse will touch us all throughout the course of our lifetime. These abusers look and speak just like us but have insidious intentions with our affections. Learning to spot emotional abuse is an imperative skill set. You have armed yourself with the knowledge required to pick a narcissist out of a crowd, and you are now equipped to stop abusers in their tracks. Remember that our bodies often know that something is wrong, long before we do.

If you or a loved one has suffered at the hands of a narcissistic partner, healing these wounds can be one of the most important moves you make toward personal evolution. Emotional trauma has the ability to wash away our motivation and sense of self, but this is not a permanent change.

Growing from your personal scars is paramount for evolution. Learning about the injuries that you have weathered is the first step toward changing into the person that you were meant to become. The damage that you've endured is not allowed to define you.

I really appreciate that you have taken the time to read this book, and I hope that it was better able to prepare you in the event that your path crosses with a narcissist.
Finally, if you found this book useful in any way, a review on Amazon is always appreciated!